# ONE PAN
## 100 brilliant meals

**Mari Mererid Williams**

Photography by Toby Scott

EBURY
PRESS

# CONTENTS

The humble frying pan – every kitchen has one! We fry our onions in it, we get it out when making a full English and we use it at least once a year on Pancake Day. But could we do more with it?

Here we have adapted family favourites and created new recipes – and all you need is a frying pan. So give your saucepan a break, your baking tins a holiday and, more importantly, cut down on the washing up.

# BEST PANS FOR THE JOB

—

Before you buy any pan (and this goes for any piece of kitchen kit) think about what your needs are. You want a pan that is large enough, but not so big that it dries out and spoils your food. Also, think about the depth of the pan. A deep pan should be deep enough to make a stir fry, stew or curry, while shallow pans are perfect for cooking crêpes and omelettes.

Whatever type of frying pan you buy, it should be sturdy. Thickness means that a pan will not dent, warp or have hot spots (which cause food in one area of the pan to cook faster or burn before everything else is done). Thinner materials can't hold heat evenly, can buckle and then won't sit level on the hob. A deeper pan should hold heat all the way up the sides; a weighty one will also be more durable and withstand frequent use and washing.

### DEEP FRYING PAN

A large deep frying pan, sometimes called a skillet or sauté pan, is the true workhorse of the kitchen. Perfect for browning large quantities of vegetables or meat, it's also excellent for braising and reducing sauces. It should have a tight-fitting lid and is often ovenproof (always check before buying, see page 8).

If you are a frying pan purist there is a difference between a sauté pan and a skillet and it's all to do with the shape. A sauté pan, from the French verb *sauter*, meaning 'to jump', has a wide flat bottom and relatively tall, vertical sides. A skillet, on the other hand, has sides that flare outwards at an angle. The sloping sides of a skillet allow you to shake the pan easily, performing the jump-flip action chefs are so keen to demonstrate. But this is more than just a flamboyant manoeuvre – it's the most efficient way to redistribute the food in the pan, ensuring even cooking of the ingredients. Messy when practising, but a skill worth conquering.

## CAST IRON PAN

The kitchen heavyweight and a true favourite of our friends across the pond. Cast iron frying pans are a little bit like AGA cooking – you either love it or hate it, and if you love it you really love it. I have to admit I got rid of my cast iron pans; I just found them too heavy and cumbersome to use. Cast iron frying pans are relatively inexpensive to buy and a well-cared-for pan will stay loyal; if you use it and care for it properly, it will only get better with age and time.

During cooking, oil bonds to the surface of cast iron, making its surface increasingly non-stick. This process is known as seasoning. A newly purchased cast iron frying pan, even if it is pre-seasoned, isn't going to have great non-stick qualities. Be sure to clean it thoroughly, scrubbing it with hot water and salt, then season it a few times by heating it over a large burner to dry, using a towel to saturate the surface with oil, and popping it into a hot oven for 20–30 minutes. Cook with it frequently, and with some patience, and you'll begin to see better non-stick results. It's essential to clean cast iron cookware properly. Once you've cooked with it, rinse it under hot water, scrubbing gently with a brush. Soap isn't really necessary. Never, ever soak a cast iron pan in the sink or it will rust. Instead wash and dry it immediately, and then put it on the burner to dry well. Once it's fully dry, add a few drops of oil and swirl to coat the pan, wipe away with kitchen paper until you've rubbed all excess oil off the pan.

Once the pan is well seasoned, you will need less oil than in a regular pan – and the more you cook with your cast iron, the better it will perform. Cast iron pans heat up slowly, but will hold their temperature well and conduct heat evenly. They are brilliant at cooking pizzas, frying chicken, crisping bacon and baking bread.

## NON-STICK

If your cast iron pan is years old, well used and seasoned, it should be non-stick. But sometimes you just need ease and the guarantee of a non-stick pan. If you can only afford one pan, opt for a general-purpose non-stick one. It will see you through most cooking tasks and is a breeze to clean up. To make the greatest use of it, buy a pan that is ovenproof. Whatever the manufacturers claim, only use wooden or silicone or plastic utensils on it to protect the non-stick surface and prolong its life.

## SHALLOW FLAT PAN

These are not as versatile as deeper pans but are ideal for making pancakes, omelettes or rösti.

## CHECK THE PANS ARE OVENPROOF

In many recipes you start the cooking process on the hob and then transfer it to the oven or under the grill. The entire frying pan should be ovenproof, including the handle. An ovenproof frying pan means you can serve many of the dishes in this book straight to the table, but remember the pan will be hot so make sure you have a heatproof mat at the ready.

# MY PANS OF CHOICE

My frying pans of choice and those used to test the recipes in this book were: one large deep 28cm (11in) wide sauté pan with a lid – it's one I have had for years, so is well seasoned and dependable; also two stainless steel non-stick ovenproof skillets measuring 20cm (8in) and 24cm (9½in). They are deep skillet/sauté hybrids, giving you the capacity of the sauté pan with a slight curved edge, but at the same time offering you the tossing ability of the skillet. The non-stick surface ensures the ingredients won't stick to the pans, even the cakes! This also allows an easy, quick clean up. All three pans have worked hard for me and I loved testing and adapting recipes to work in them.

# CARE AND CLEANING

Take care of your pans. Check the manufacturer booklet in case they have specific instructions, otherwise follow these simple rules and your pans will last longer.

* Never leave an empty pan on the heat or in a hot oven.
* However tempting, do not put a hot pan straight into water. It can cause warping and damage the non-stick coating. If the pan is warped it gives an uneven distribution of heat. Leave the pan to cool and then wash.
* Whatever the manufacturer claims, try not to put the pan in the dishwasher but, if you must, dry it properly. Wash the pan by hand with soapy water. Do not use scouring pads as again, this can damage the non-stick coating.
* Use high temperature silicone utensils for non-stick pans. Some frying pan brands suggest you can use metal utensils with their non-stick pans but this is not recommended as you are more likely to damage the non-stick surface.
* When stacking the pans place a sheet of baking paper between them. This protects the surfaces from scratches.

## TIPS ON CLEANING BURNT PANS

It happens to us all – a knock on the door, we get lost in social media and oops, it's burnt. The dish may be beyond redemption but don't condemn the pan to the same destiny.

Fill the base of the pan with a layer of water and 250ml (9floz) vinegar and bring the pan to the boil. It should be looking a bit cleaner already. Remove the pan from the heat and add 2 tablespoons bicarbonate of soda. It may fizz so step back. Leave for 5 minutes. Empty the pan and clean as normal.

Or even easier: fill the burnt pan with water and add a dishwasher tablet or 1 tablespoon biological washing powder. Bring to the boil. Leave to simmer for around 10 minutes and the burnt bits will simply lift away, leaving your pan as good as new. Repeat as necessary, and then wash thoroughly as normal.

# OTHER USES FOR A FRYING PAN

—

BAKE

Just think of your frying pan as a cake tin. If your pan is non-stick you don't need to line the pan. However, popping two strips of baking paper across the bottom of the pan does make it easier to lift the cake out of the pan (see Plum Cake, page 156). If the recipe calls for the mixing to be done in the frying pan as well as the cooking, use either a wooden spoon or a plastic spatula. Crumbles and cobblers work especially well in a frying pan as you can stew the fruits in the pan, developing the delicious juices and flavours. Top with either the crumble or cobbler and pop in the oven. Bake and serve in the pan when ready.

ROAST AND TOAST

**NUTS**
Simply pour the nuts into a dry pan and place over a medium heat. Shake the pan to flatten the nuts into a single layer. Once you can smell the nuts toasting, toss the nuts to turn and shake the pan again to spread them out in a single layer. Toss and shake 3–4 times to make sure the nuts are toasted on all sides, then pour them onto a plate lined with kitchen paper to cool. This process should take 5 minutes or so. Don't take your eyes off the pan or you'll find yourself throwing a pan full of burnt and bitter nuts in the bin.

**SPICES**
Pour the whole spices into a dry pan and place over a medium heat. Stir and toss them around for 1–2 minutes, or until they begin to look toasted and start to jump in the pan. Transfer them to a pestle and mortar, crush them to a powder or coarsely grind them according to the recipe instructions. This will be easier to do now that they have been roasted.

CRUSH AND
FLATTEN

**MEAT**
Use the frying pan to tenderise and flatten meat. Simply place the fillets between two sheets of cling film and use the weight of the pan to flatten them out (see Pan Fried Chicken Caesar Salad with Charred Lettuce, page 126).

**BISCUITS**
Put biscuits into a plastic bag and cover with a tea towel. Use the weight of the pan to bash the biscuits, until they are finely crushed.

**GARLIC**
Place garlic on to a chopping board and smash with the bottom of a pan.

# TOO HOT TO HANDLE
## LAST IMPORTANT NOTE!
—

REMEMBER that every time you remove the pan from the oven the handle will be hot. BE CAREFUL – either use a pot cloth or a handle cover. You can buy silicone or fabric handle covers that you slip on the handle before removing from the oven. Remember to leave the cover on the handle until the handle is cool to the touch, or cover the handle with a tea towel. Chefs apparently throw flour over a hot handle to identify it as a hot handle. I cover mine with a tea towel to remind myself and the family that it is still hot. This is important especially if you are serving the dish straight to the table.

**With many of us trying to edit our lives and reduce the amount of 'things' we have in the house, take a look in your kitchen cupboards – are they ready for a declutter? How many of those pots and pans do you actually use on a day-to-day basis? Are there any you could do without, especially now you have been introduced to the new-found use of the humble frying pan?**

# CONVERSION TABLES

## WEIGHTS

| METRIC | IMPERIAL | METRIC | IMPERIAL |
|--------|----------|--------|----------|
| 15 g | ½ oz | 300 g | 11 oz |
| 25 g | 1 oz | 350 g | 12 oz |
| 40 g | 1½ oz | 375 g | 13 oz |
| 50 g | 2 oz | 400 g | 14 oz |
| 75 g | 3 oz | 425 g | 15 oz |
| 100 g | 4 oz | 450 g | 1 lb |
| 150 g | 5 oz | 550 g | 1¼ lb |
| 175 g | 6 oz | 675 g | 1½ lb |
| 200 g | 7 oz | 900 g | 2 lb |
| 225 g | 8 oz | 1.5 kg | 3 lb |
| 250 g | 9 oz | 1.75 kg | 4 lb |
| 275 g | 10 oz | 2.25 kg | 5 lb |

## VOLUME

| METRIC | IMPERIAL | METRIC | IMPERIAL |
|--------|----------|--------|----------|
| 25 ml | 1 fl oz | 1.25 litres | 2¼ pints |
| 50 ml | 2 fl oz | 1.5 litres | 2½ pints |
| 85 ml | 3 fl oz | 1.6 litres | 2¾ pints |
| 150 ml | 5 fl oz (¼ pint) | 1.75 litres | 3 pints |
| 300 ml | 10 fl oz (½ pint) | 1.8 litres | 3¼ pints |
| 400 ml | 14 fl oz | 2 litres | 3½ pints |
| 450 ml | 15 fl oz (¾ pint) | 2.1 litres | 3¾ pints |
| 600 ml | 1 pint | 2.25 litres | 4 pints |
| 700 ml | 1¼ pints | 2.75 litres | 5 pints |
| 900 ml | 1½ pints | 3.4 litres | 6 pints |
| 1 litres | 1¾ pints | 3.9 litres | 7 pints |
| 1.2 litres | 2 pints | 5 litres | 8 pints (1 gal) |

# MEASUREMENTS

| METRIC | IMPERIAL |
| --- | --- |
| 0.5 cm | ¼ inch |
| 1 cm | ½ inch |
| 2.5 cm | 1 inch |
| 5 cm | 2 inches |
| 7.5 cm | 3 inches |
| 10 cm | 4 inches |
| 15 cm | 6 inches |
| 18 cm | 7 inches |
| 20 cm | 8 inches |
| 23 cm | 9 inches |
| 25 cm | 10 inches |
| 30 cm | 12 inches |

# OVEN TEMPERATURES

| °C | °F | GAS MK |
| --- | --- | --- |
| 140°C | 275°F | 1 |
| 150°C | 300°F | 2 |
| 160°C | 325°F | 3 |
| 180°C | 350°F | 4 |
| 190°C | 375°F | 5 |
| 200°C | 400°F | 6 |
| 220°C | 425°F | 7 |
| 230°C | 450°F | 8 |
| 240°C | 475°F | 9 |

# BREAKFASTS

# BANJO SANDWICH:
## *the* ULTIMATE EGG *and* BACON SANDWICH

**SERVES 2**

🥄 5 mins

🍳 15 mins

2 tbsp vegetable oil

8 rashers back bacon

2 medium eggs

1 tbsp tomato ketchup

1 tsp Dijon mustard

A few drops hot chilli sauce (optional)

25g (1oz) butter, softened

4 slices medium sliced white bread

**So called a Banjo Sandwich because, when you bite into it the yolk and sauce dribble down your front; you move the hand holding the sandwich away from you to avoid further spillage and attempt to wipe the dribbled yolk away with a banjo playing kind of action. This sandwich is one of life's simple pleasures.**

1. Heat the oil in a 24cm (9½in) non-stick frying pan. Add the bacon and cook over a medium heat for 3–4 minutes until the fat is beginning to crisp. When the bacon is cooked to your liking, drain on kitchen paper and keep warm.

2. Increase the heat to medium-high, then break each egg into the pan and leave for about 30 seconds to begin to set. When the white looks almost set, turn the heat down low and using a metal spoon, baste the eggs all over with the fat in the pan. The yolk will cook lightly on top and become opaque. For a more well done egg, flip it over using a palette knife or fish slice and cook for 5–10 seconds.

3. Mix together the tomato ketchup, Dijon mustard and chilli sauce, if using.

4. Butter two slices of bread and spread the ketchup mix on the other two slices. Divide the bacon between two buttered bread slices and drain the eggs on kitchen paper before placing them on top. Season, then cover with the remaining bread and serve. Remember napkins are essential!

# ALL-IN-ONE FARMER'S BREAKFAST

2–3 tbsp sunflower oil

4 chipolata sausages

3 rashers smoked bacon

2 portobello mushrooms, sliced

1 x 200g (7oz) can chopped tomatoes

1 x 200g (7oz) can baked beans

1 tsp chilli flakes (optional)

2 eggs (or more if you want)

Handful of parsley, chopped

Salt and pepper

Buttered toast, to serve

**There is very little that can beat a good, hearty full English breakfast but, and it's a very big but, it creates a lot of washing up! Try this all-in-one version. Serve to share, with two forks and lots of white buttered toast.**

1. Heat the oil in a large 28cm (11in) frying pan and add the sausages. Cook for 5–6 minutes, turning regularly until the sausages are light golden brown. Add the bacon and mushrooms and fry for a further 3–5 minutes until browned.

2. Add the tinned tomatoes, baked beans and chilli flakes, if using, and bring to a gentle bubble.

3. Once the sausages are cooked, make two spaces in the mixture and crack in the eggs. Cover and simmer on low for 3–4 minutes until the whites are cooked but the yolks are still runny.

4. Sprinkle with parsley, salt and pepper and serve with a pile of hot buttered white toast.

# HEARTY BREAKFAST

SERVES 2

10 mins

30 mins

2 tbsp coconut oil

4 slices unsmoked bacon, chopped

½ red onion, sliced

4 sausages

200g (7oz) butternut squash, peeled and spiralised or grated

300g (11oz) baby spinach, washed and trimmed

4 medium eggs

Salt and pepper

**This has many of my favourite ingredients – bacon, sausage, butternut squash and spinach – and is certainly a dish to set you up for the day. Leave out the bacon and sausage and replace with peppers and courgettes for a vegetarian version. You can buy shredded or spiralised vegetables in the supermarket now, which makes this dish even easier to prepare.**

1. Heat a deep 28cm (11in) frying pan and add the coconut oil. Cook the bacon until it begins to colour. Add the onion and cook until the onion is soft and translucent and the bacon is colouring nicely.

2. Run a sharp knife down the centre of the sausages, gently peel off the skin and discard. Break up the sausage-meat with your hands and add to the frying pan. Cook for about 5–10 minutes, or until the sausage is brown and has a crust forming.

3. Add the butternut squash and cook for about 3–5 minutes. Add the spinach and cook for a further 3 minutes, or until wilted. Press small pockets into the mixture. Crack the eggs into each of the pockets, being careful not to break the yolks.

4. Cook for about 5 minutes, or until the eggs are done to your liking. Season and serve.

# PIPERADE SCRAMBLED EGG

2 tbsp olive oil

1 onion, chopped

1 red pepper, deseeded and diced

1 green pepper, deseeded and diced

1 ripe tomato, peeled, deseeded and roughly chopped

2 garlic cloves, finely chopped

Pinch of chilli flakes (optional)

6 large eggs, lightly beaten

1 tsp thyme leaves

Salt and pepper

Thick buttered toast, to serve

4 slices prosciutto, to serve

**This takes the humble scrambled eggs to another level. You could add chorizo, bacon or even fresh chilli. Do not overcook or the scrambled egg will become rubbery rather than soft and silky.**

1. Heat the olive oil in a 24cm (9½in) non-stick frying pan over a medium heat.

2. Add the onion and peppers and cook gently for 10 minutes, or until the vegetables are soft.

3. Add the tomato, garlic and chilli flakes, if using, and cook until warmed through and the tomato juices have evaporated.

4. Season the beaten eggs and add to the vegetables. Stir with a wooden spoon, lifting and folding the egg from the bottom of the pan. Repeat until the eggs are softly set and slightly runny in places. Remove from the heat and leave for a few seconds to finish cooking. Sprinkle with the thyme.

5. Serve on thick buttered toast, topped with the prosciutto.

# SMOKED SALMON BREAKFAST FRITTATA

200g (7oz) baby spinach

1 tbsp olive oil

200g (7oz) asparagus tips

6 eggs

2 tbsp crème fraîche

2 tbsp dill, chopped

100g (4oz) smoked salmon, cut into wide strips

2 tbsp soft cheese

**Smoked salmon and dill give this frittata a distinctive flavour, but you can adapt the recipe to use whatever you happen to have in the fridge. Perfect for breakfast, delicious for lunch and very welcome on a picnic.**

1. Preheat the grill to medium-high.

2. Heat a 20cm (8in) non-stick ovenproof frying pan. Add the spinach and a tablespoon of water and wilt for 30 seconds. Drain the spinach in a colander and season well. Wipe the frying pan with kitchen paper.

3. Heat the oil in the pan and add the asparagus. Cook for 4–5 minutes, or until they start to colour.

4. Whisk the eggs, crème fraîche and dill (reserving a little to garnish) in a jug and stir in the salmon.

5. Return the spinach to the frying pan and pour the egg mixture over the asparagus and spinach, shaking the pan gently so the egg mixture spreads into all the holes. Dot over the soft cheese. Scatter with the reserved dill and then cook over a low heat for 8–10 minutes, until it is just setting on the bottom.

6. Grill for 4–5 minutes until the top has just set. Loosen the edges with a palette knife and then slide on to a plate. Cut into wedges and serve either hot or warm.

# SHAKSHUKA

10 mins

50 mins

2 tbsp olive oil

1 onion, sliced

1 large red pepper, deseeded and sliced

1 large yellow pepper, deseeded and sliced

3 garlic cloves, finely chopped

1 tsp paprika

2 tbsp harissa paste

2 x 400g (14oz) cans chopped tomatoes

1 tbsp tomato purée

1 tsp sugar

4 medium eggs

Salt and pepper

Handful coriander, roughly chopped

**A delicious Middle Eastern dish with the added twist of harissa spice mix. Traditionally served for breakfast but good enough to eat at any time of day.**

1. Heat the oil in a large 26cm (10¼in) lidded frying pan over a medium heat and add the onion. Cook for 8–10 minutes, or until the onion starts to colour. Add the peppers and cook until both are soft, then stir in the garlic, paprika and harissa paste. Cook for another couple of minutes.

2. Add the tomatoes, tomato purée and sugar and bring to the boil. Reduce the heat and simmer for 30 minutes. Taste and season.

3. Make four pockets in the sauce and break in the eggs. Season them lightly, turn the heat down as low as possible, cover and cook for about 7 minutes, or until the eggs are just set. Sprinkle with coriander and serve with lots of sourdough to mop up the delicious juices.

# SPICED HOB GRANOLA

2 tbsp coconut oil

150g (5oz) jumbo rolled oats

75g (3oz) seeds such as pumpkin, sunflower

150g (5oz) mixed nuts (such as pistachios, pecans, almonds), chopped if necessary

55g (2¼oz) flaked coconut

2 tbsp desiccated coconut

3 tbsp honey or maple syrup

Pinch of salt

1 tsp ground cinnamon

½ tsp ground cardamom

1 tsp ground ginger

1 tsp ground allspice

½ tsp nutmeg

75g (3oz) chia seeds

75g (3oz) dried cranberries or cherries

**You can tailor-make homemade granola to include your favourite ingredients so add seeds, nuts and spices to suit your taste. The key here is patience: do not rush the toasting or you will have a burnt offering on your hands.**

1. Heat a large frying pan over a medium heat and melt the coconut oil. Add the oats, seeds, nuts and both coconuts. Stir well so that they are coated in oil. Drizzle with the honey or maple syrup and mix to combine. Press into one single layer covering the bottom of the frying pan.

2. Cook for 5–10 minutes, stirring occasionally, but making sure to press the mixture back down into the pan after it's been stirred. You are looking for lightly browned oats and a wonderful toasted, not burnt, aroma.

3. Stir in the salt and spices and cook for a further minute. Turn off the heat and add the chia seeds and cranberries. Toss to combine, before pressing it into a single layer in the pan again. Leave until cool and store in an airtight container. Serve with yoghurt and fresh fruits.

# TOASTED PORRIDGE TOPPED *with* FIGS *and* CARAMELISED NUTS

SERVES 2

🥄 20 mins

🍲 30 mins

## FOR THE FIG TOPPING:

2 tbsp orange juice

2 fresh figs

1 tbsp dried cranberries

## FOR THE CARAMELISED NUTS AND SEEDS:

50g (2oz) mixed nuts

2 tbsp mixed seeds

3 tbsp maple syrup

Pinch of sea salt

## FOR THE TOASTED PORRIDGE:

100g (4oz) jumbo oats

200ml (7floz) whole milk

400ml (14floz) water

Generous pinch of salt

**Toasting gives oats a slight crisp texture and an enhanced nutty flavour. If figs are not available serve with stewed apples, plums or dried fruit.**

1. **For the fig topping**: heat the orange juice in a large deep 24cm (9½in) non-stick frying pan and add the figs and dried cranberries. Cook for 5 minutes, or until the figs have softened and the dried cranberries have puffed up slightly. Pour into a bowl and wipe the pan clean.

2. **For the maple-caramelised nuts and seeds**: heat the pan over a medium heat until hot. Add the nuts, seeds, maple syrup and salt and stir constantly for 2–3 minutes until the nuts and seeds are coated and the mixture is thick and reduced. Remove and set aside to use later. Wash the pan.

3. **For the toasted porridge**: heat the frying pan over a medium-high heat and add the oats. Toast the oats until fragrant and with a hint of colour. Add the milk and water and bring slowly to the boil, stirring frequently.

4. Turn down the heat to the lowest setting and simmer, stirring regularly, for about 10 minutes, until you have the consistency you require. After about 5 minutes, add the salt.

5. Remove from the heat and allow to sit for 5 minutes. Serve topped with the figs and the caramelised nuts and seeds.

🥄 10 mins

🍲 20 mins

# BRIOCHE FRENCH TOAST

4–6 slices brioche

2 tsp sugar

½ tsp ground cinnamon

⅛ tsp grated nutmeg

1 large egg

60ml (2½ floz) milk (or cream, if you happen to have some in your fridge)

Zest and juice of ½ orange

2 large knobs butter

Berries and crème fraîche, to serve

**This rich breakfast or brunch dish is always a crowd-pleaser. Make with leftover panettone at Christmas, or just plain white bread.**

1. You could start this the night before by leaving the brioche slices uncovered so they dry out a little. If the brioche loaf is slightly stale already you do not need to do this.

2. Mix together the sugar, cinnamon and nutmeg in a small bowl.

3. Whisk together the egg, milk (or cream), orange zest and juice in a bowl then transfer into a shallow dish big enough to hold the brioche slices. Add the brioche and soak for about 30 seconds each side.

4. Melt half the butter in a 24cm (9½in) non-stick frying pan. When the butter is melted and just foaming, add the soaked brioche and cook for 2–3 minutes on the first side, or until it's golden brown; adjust the heat so it's not cooking too slowly or too quickly. Turn the toast over, and cook the second side until golden brown, about 2 minutes. Repeat with remaining butter and slices. Once cooked, sprinkle the brioche with the cinnamon sugar.

5. Serve with lots of berries and crème fraîche.

# FRUITED SODA BREAD

MAKES 1 LOAF

5 mins

50 mins

25g (1oz) butter

50g (2oz) rolled oats, plus a handful for sprinkling

200g (7oz) wholemeal flour

300g (11oz) plain flour

½ tsp salt

1 level tsp bicarbonate of soda

1½ tsp mixed spice

1 tbsp treacle

1 tbsp honey

450ml (15floz) buttermilk

75g (3oz) mixed dried fruit

1 tbsp melted butter, to finish

**This bread is equally delicious eaten as a savoury with cheese or just buttered and enjoyed with a cup of tea. Swap the mixed dried fruit for dried sour cherries or cranberries. The heavy base of the frying pan will help to give the loaf a well-baked crust all round.**

1. Preheat the oven to 200°C, fan oven 180°C, Gas mark 6.

2. Dust a 20cm (8in) ovenproof frying pan with flour and place a circle of baking paper in the base.

3. Rub together the butter and oats in a large bowl. Add the flours, salt, bicarbonate of soda and mixed spice and stir together. Make a well in the middle.

4. Stir the treacle and honey into the buttermilk until well mixed, then pour this into the well and very quickly stir together until you have a soft, sticky dough. Add the dried fruit and mix until the fruit is well distributed.

5. Tip on to a lightly floured surface and fold into a round ball and sprinkle with the oats. Put into the prepared frying pan and cut a cross in the top.

6. Bake in the oven for 50 minutes to 1 hour, keeping an eye on it, until the crust is golden and the loaf sounds hollow when tapped underneath.

7. Brush with melted butter and leave to cool before tearing into it. Eat as soon as possible, as it doesn't keep very well.

10 mins

30 mins

# BREAKFAST QUINOA BANANA BAKE

1 tbsp coconut oil

170g (6oz) red and white quinoa, thoroughly rinsed and shaken dry

200ml (7floz) coconut milk (make sure you have mixed it well before measuring)

250ml (9floz) hot water

¼ tsp salt

100g (4oz or approx 7) medjool dates, pitted and chopped

35g (1¼oz) desiccated coconut

1 medium banana, peeled and diagonally sliced

1 tsp ground cinnamon

100g (4oz) pecans, coarsely chopped

Thick Greek yoghurt, to serve

**A crunchy alternative to porridge. Add fruits, nuts or seeds of your choice to make this a great start for the day.**

1. Preheat the oven to 190°C, fan oven 170°C, Gas mark 5.

2. Heat the coconut oil in a 24cm (9½in) ovenproof frying pan. Add the quinoa and stir to coat the grains. Cook for 3 minutes then add the coconut milk, water and salt and bring to the boil over a high heat.

3. Reduce the heat to low, cover and simmer for 10 minutes. Add the dates, desiccated coconut, banana and half the cinnamon. Stir well and remove the pan from the heat.

4. Combine the pecans and remaining cinnamon in a small bowl and scatter the mixture over the quinoa. Bake uncovered in the oven for 20 minutes until the top is golden brown. Serve warm with a large dollop of cold Greek yoghurt.

# POTATO, CHORIZO
## *and* CHEESE OMELETTE

**SERVES 1**

5 mins

10 mins

3 large eggs

50g (2oz) chorizo sausages, sliced

2 small cooked potatoes, cut into chunks

2 spring onions, thinly sliced

25g (1oz) strong Cheddar cheese, grated

1 tsp thyme leaves

Salt and pepper

**Master the simple omelette and you will never go hungry. You can use many ingredients as filling – peppers, courgettes, peas, ham – the list is endless.**

1. Beat the eggs with a fork in a jug and season lightly.

2. Heat a 20cm (8in) non-stick ovenproof frying pan. Add the chorizo and potato and cook until the chorizo has released its delicious red oil and the potatoes are turning a crisp golden colour.

3. Remove the chorizo and potato from the pan with a slotted spoon and put to one side. Pour most of the oil away leaving a film of oil over the base of the pan. Heat again.

4. Pour in the beaten eggs and cook for 2 minutes. Move the pan around and stir to spread the eggs evenly. When the egg starts to cook and begins to firm up, but still has a little raw egg on top, add the chorizo, potatoes, spring onions and cheese to one side of the omelette. Sprinkle with the thyme.

5. When the eggs have set fold the omelette in half. Tilt the frying pan slightly to move the omelette to the edge of the pan. Slide on to a plate and serve.

🔪 10 mins

🍲 25 mins

# SWEET POTATO PANCAKES *topped with* BLACK BEAN *and* CHORIZO *with* AVOCADO YOGHURT

FOR THE PANCAKES:

140g (5oz) plain flour

½ tsp bicarbonate of soda

½ tsp nutmeg

½ tsp ground ginger

1 egg, beaten

370ml (13floz) buttermilk

160g (5½oz) cooked sweet potato, mashed

1–2 tbsp coconut oil

FOR THE BLACK BEAN TOPPING:

1 x 400g (14oz) can black beans, drained

½ tsp ground cumin

½ tsp dried oregano

1 tsp dried chilli flakes

2 spring onions, sliced

1 red pepper, deseeded and diced

80g (3½oz) Cheddar or Monterey Jack, grated

150g (5oz) chorizo, cubed

Lime wedges, to serve

FOR THE AVOCADO YOGHURT:

1 ripe avocado

100g (4oz) Greek yoghurt

Fresh coriander, chopped

**The sweetness of the pancakes topped with slight chilli heat of the bean mix and the cool silky texture of the avocado yoghurt makes a winning lunch or brunch combination. These pancakes could also be served piled high with berries, a large dollop of Greek yoghurt and a drizzle of honey.**

1. Mix together the flour, bicarbonate of soda, nutmeg and ginger. Make a well in the middle and add the egg and buttermilk. Whisk together until you get a smooth batter. Add the mashed sweet potato and stir it in gently, distributing it evenly throughout the batter. Don't worry too much about any lumps.

2. Heat a large 26cm (10¼in) non-stick frying pan, add the coconut oil and heat until it sizzles, then pour it out into a little bowl to use again. Reduce the heat to low and pour 2 large tablespoons of batter on to the pan (use a metal ring if you want to get them perfect). Cook for 2–3 minutes or until the underside is golden brown and bubbles appear on the top. Flip and cook for another couple of minutes. Cook the pancakes individually or in batches. Repeat until all the batter is used, adding the coconut oil to the pan again, if necessary. Keep the pancakes warm under foil while you make the topping.

3. Mix the beans, cumin, oregano, chilli, spring onions, pepper and cheese together in a bowl. Heat 1 teaspoon of coconut oil in the frying pan over a medium heat. Add the chorizo and fry for 3–4 minutes until crisp. Add the bean mix and heat gently.

4. Mash the avocado and add to the yoghurt. Stir in the coriander.

5. Serve the sweet potato pancakes topped with the bean mix, a generous squeeze of lime and a spoonful of the avocado yoghurt.

# SALTED CARAMEL *and* CHOCOLATE PANCAKE STACK

SERVES 4

🥄 20 mins, plus 30 mins
   to rest batter

🍲 25 mins

**FOR THE PANCAKES:**

125g (4½oz) plain flour

Pinch of salt

1 egg plus 1 egg yolk

225ml (8floz) milk

2 tbsp water

Small knob of butter

**FOR SALTED CARAMEL SAUCE:**

75g (3oz) unsalted butter

50g (2oz) soft light brown sugar

50g (2oz) caster sugar

50g (2oz) golden syrup

125ml (4½floz) double cream

1 tsp sea salt

75g (3oz) chocolate, dark or milk, grated

Crème fraîche, to serve (optional)

**Who can resist the perfect combination of pancakes, salted caramel and chocolate? The pancakes could be cooked before hand, interleaved with baking paper and wrapped in cling film and frozen. When ready to use, leave to defrost until you can separate and then carry on with the stacking. Of course you could also use ready-made bought caramel sauce.**

1. Preheat the oven to 180°C, fan oven 160°C, Gas mark 4.

2. Sift the flour into a large mixing bowl and add the salt. Make a well in the middle of the flour and break in the whole egg and egg yolk.

3. Whisk together the milk and water and pour half over the eggs. Start whisking from the centre, gradually drawing the flour into the eggs and milk. Once all the flour is incorporated, beat until you have a smooth, thick paste. Add a little more milk if it is too stiff to beat. Whisk the remaining milk into the batter until it is the consistency of thick single cream. Cover and refrigerate for at least 30 minutes.

4. Heat a 20cm (8in) non-stick ovenproof frying pan over a medium heat and add the butter – you only need enough to grease the base of the pan. Ladle some batter into the pan and tilt the pan around for a thin even coverage. When it begins to set, loosen the edges with a thin spatula or palette knife, and when it begins to colour on the bottom, flip it over and cook for another 30 seconds. Continue with the rest of the batter, stacking the pancakes on to a plate.

5. When all the pancakes are cooked, wipe the pan and make the salted caramel sauce.

6. Put the butter, sugars and syrup in the pan and simmer for 3 minutes, swirling every now and again. Add the cream and half a teaspoon of salt and swirl again; give it a stir with a wooden spoon. Spoon out some of the mixture and when cool enough, taste and check the salt level.

7. Place the first pancake in the frying pan, then pile the pancakes up drizzling the caramel sauce over each pancake and sprinkling with grated chocolate before adding the next one. Continue stacking until you have used all the pancakes, chocolate and sauce. Place in the oven for 10 minutes until the chocolate is melted. Serve in wedges topped with crème fraîche.

# BERRY FILLED DUTCH BABY

3 large eggs

1 tbsp caster sugar

150ml (5floz) whole milk

100g (4oz) plain flour

1 tsp vanilla bean paste

Pinch of salt

¼ tsp freshly grated nutmeg

15g (½oz) butter

A selection of berries and icing sugar, to serve

**A cross between Yorkshire pudding and pancake, this light fluffy dish can be topped with sweet or savoury goodies. If you want to be fancy, buy individual frying pans and serve one per person. You could serve with lemon curd, peanut butter or even bacon.**

1. Preheat the oven to 220°C, fan oven 200°C, Gas mark 7.

2. Place a 20cm (8in) ovenproof frying pan (or four smaller pans if making individual ones) into the oven to heat up while you prepare the batter.

3. Put the eggs, sugar, milk, flour, vanilla, salt and nutmeg into a food processor or blender and whizz until smooth and lump-free.

4. Very carefully and wearing thick oven mitts, remove the pan from the oven. Add the butter and swirl the pan to melt the butter and coat the base and sides of the pan. If you think the pan has cooled down too much just heat up gently on the hob until the butter just starts to sizzle.

5. Pour in the batter – it should sizzle as it hits the pan. Tilt the pan if needed so that the batter runs evenly to all sides. Quickly return to the oven and cook, leaving undisturbed, for 20–25 minutes until it has puffed up like a giant Yorkshire pudding and is deep golden brown. The Dutch baby may well collapse once out of the oven, so do not be disappointed when this happens. Serve filled with berries and dusted with icing sugar.

# SNACKS

# BABA GANOUSH

**SERVES 4**

🥄 5 mins

🍲 30 mins

2 large aubergines

2 garlic cloves, crushed

Juice of ½ lemon

3 tbsp olive oil

1 tbsp tahini

1 tsp ground cumin

1 tbsp chopped parsley

1 tbsp chopped mint

Seeds of ½ large pomegranate

Salt and pepper

**It is worth persevering with slowly cooking the aubergines in the pan as it gives the flesh a wonderful smoky flavour, which makes baba ganoush a dish of deliciousness.**

1. Place a heavy-based frying pan over a high heat. Let it get smoking-hot before adding the aubergines.

2. Place the aubergines in the hot pan and cook for about 10 minutes before giving them a quarter turn with tongs. Cook for another 5–10 minutes and give them another quarter turn, and so on until the aubergines are very tender, this could take about 30 minutes.

3. Switch the heat off, cover the pan with foil and leave the aubergines to cool slightly. Once they are cool enough to handle, cut them in half and scoop the flesh out into a sieve or colander; leave to drain for 30 minutes. Spoon the flesh into a large bowl and add the garlic, lemon juice, 2 tablespoons olive oil, tahini, cumin, half a teaspoon of salt and a good grind of black pepper. Stir and allow the aubergine to marinate at room temperature for at least 1 hour.

4. Add most of the herbs and check the seasoning. Spoon into a bowl and serve drizzled with remaining olive oil and scattered with the pomegranate seeds and the remaining herbs. Delicious with warm flatbreads.

# CARAMELISED ONION DIP

2 tbsp olive oil

1 brown onion, sliced

1 red onion, sliced

1 large garlic clove, crushed

1 tbsp Worcestershire sauce

2 sprigs fresh thyme

200g (7oz) full fat Greek yoghurt

Salt and pepper

**The wonderful sweet onions coupled with the fresh sharp yoghurt make a wonder dip. If possible make this the day before so the flavours really develop.**

1. Heat the oil in a deep frying pan. Add the onions and cook for 15 minutes over a medium heat, stirring every now and again, until the onions caramelise into a deep brown colour.

2. Add the garlic and stir for several seconds until you can smell it. Turn off the heat and stir in the Worcestershire sauce. Strip the leaves from the thyme and add to the onions. Leave to cool.

3. Mix the cooled onions and the yoghurt until blended. Season to taste. Chill for at least 1 hour and serve with toasted sourdough fingers.

# ROASTED RED PEPPER
## *and* WALNUT DIP

**SERVES 4**

🥄 10 mins

🍳 20 mins

3 large red peppers, halved and deseeded

100g (4oz) walnuts

½ tsp ground cumin

¼ tsp paprika

¼ tsp cayenne pepper

2 garlic cloves, crushed

2 tbsp olive oil

2 tsp pomegranate molasses

Zest and juice of ½ lemon

½ tsp coarse sea salt

Handful of fresh parsley, chopped

4 pitta breads

**Otherwise known as Muhammara, this smoky red pepper dip is good on the day of making but is even better the next day.**

1. Place a heavy-based frying pan over a high heat. Let it get smoking-hot before adding the peppers, skin side down, to the hot pan.

2. Reduce the heat and cook until the skins are black and charred. Place the charred peppers into a plastic bag and seal.

3. Return the pan to the heat, add the walnuts and toast until the walnuts are slightly darker in colour. Keep an eye on them as they can burn easily.

4. Once the peppers are cool enough to handle, peel the skins away. Place in the bowl of a food processor along with most of the walnuts (keep a few back to garnish) and spices. Add the garlic, 2 tablespoons of the olive oil, pomegranate molasses, lemon zest and juice. Process but keep a little texture.

5. Season with the sea salt. Place the dip in a bowl and garnish with the parsley and a couple of walnut pieces.

6. Heat a clean frying pan and add the pitta breads, toast for a couple of minutes until the pittas are golden brown. Slice into fingers and serve with the roasted pepper dip.

5 mins

10 mins

# HOME-MADE TORTILLA CHIPS

Approx 200ml (7floz) vegetable oil

8 flour tortillas, cut into 8 triangles

COATING FLAVOURS:

Paprika

Sea salt

Cinnamon and sugar

**When the family cannot agree on which flavour of tortilla chips to buy, here is your answer – make your own. Crisp, golden brown and flavoured to order.**

1. Heat the vegetable oil in a large deep heavy-based frying pan until a breadcrumb added sizzles gently. (CAUTION: hot oil can be dangerous! Do not leave unattended.)

2. Place some kitchen paper on a large plate. Place about 6 tortilla triangles in a single layer and not overlapping into the hot oil. Fry for about 2 minutes until the triangles are beginning to colour and are firm and crisp. Turn over if needed to brown evenly.

3. Using tongs or a slotted spoon, remove the triangles from the oil and place on the kitchen paper-lined plate. Sprinkle with the coating of your choice. Place more kitchen paper over the top ready for the next batch to be fried.

4. Serve with your favourite dip.

# LOADED NACHOS

SERVES 4

🥄 20 mins

🍲 10 mins

FOR THE SALSA:

2 corn on the cobs, left whole but husks removed

4 ripe tomatoes, finely chopped

1 garlic clove, finely chopped

2 tbsp finely chopped coriander

2 tbsp white wine vinegar

1 x 200g (7oz) jar sliced jalapeño chillies, drained

Pinch of sugar

Pinch of salt

FOR THE GUACAMOLE:

1 ripe avocado, flesh chopped

½ green chilli, finely chopped

½ red onion, very finely chopped

Lime juice, to taste

FOR THE NACHOS:

Home-made tortilla chips (see page 45)

100g (4oz) vintage Cheddar cheese, grated

75g (3oz) Monterey Jack

100ml (3floz) soured cream

Large handful of fresh coriander

**This is ideal cooked and served in an old beaten up frying pan, the type that you can pick up from a car boot sale. A perfect dish for those film nights.**

1. **For the salsa:** heat a large frying pan and add the corn. Cook the corn turning occasionally until browned all over. Once cool enough to handle slice off the kernels and put into a large bowl. Add the tomatoes, garlic, coriander, vinegar and half the jalapeños and season to taste with the sugar and salt.

2. **For the guacamole:** put all the ingredients into a bowl and mash with a fork until combined but not completely smooth.

3. Preheat the grill to high.

4. Pile the tortilla chips into a large frying pan and sprinkle with the cheeses, making sure there is an even distribution of cheese. Grill until the cheese is melted. Spoon over the salsa, guacamole, the soured cream and the remainder of the jalapeños. Sprinkle with lots of coriander.

# PAN ROASTED
# SPICY MIXED NUTS

2 tbsp sunflower oil

125g (4½oz) unsalted cashew nuts

125g (4½oz) unsalted almonds

125g (4½oz) unsalted macadamia nuts

1 tbsp flaky sea salt

1 tbsp sugar

½ tsp ground cumin

½ tsp dried thyme

1 rosemary sprig, leaves removed and chopped

**Use a selection of nuts but make sure they are the raw unsalted version. Your house will smell amazing when these are roasting.**

1. Heat the oil in a large frying pan. Add the nuts and toss in the hot oil. Reduce the heat and cook until they start to get golden. Do not turn your back on these as they can burn really quickly. Remove from the heat.

2. Add the rest of the ingredients and stir until everything is well coated. Toss the pan around a few times while the nuts are cooling. Perfect to eat while bingeing on the latest box set.

5 mins

5 mins

# SWEET *and* STICKY NUTS

200g (7oz) mixed raw nuts, such as pistachios, pecans, cashews, blanched almonds, blanched hazelnuts

25g (1oz) unsalted butter

1 tbsp soft light brown sugar

½ tsp mixed spice

¼ tsp ground cinnamon

½ tsp ground cardamom

1 tbsp clear honey

Sea salt, to sprinkle

**These sweet, salty, sticky nuts are easy to make and even easier to eat, especially with a refreshing G'n'T.**

1. Line a baking sheet with baking paper.

2. Heat a heavy-based frying pan and add the nuts. Toast for about 3 minutes, or until the nuts start to take on colour. Do not turn your back on them as they will burn easily. Stir in the butter, sugar, spices and honey and toss to coat evenly.

3. Cook gently for 2 minutes, stirring occasionally, or until the sugar starts to caramelise. Remove from the heat and spoon the nuts on to the prepared baking sheet. Sprinkle with the sea salt and leave to cool.

4. To serve, break into clusters and pile into a bowl.

# HONEYED SESAME SEED POPCORN

1 tbsp sunflower or vegetable oil

50g (2oz) popping corn

FLAVOURINGS:

2 tbsp black sesame seeds

2 tbsp sesame seeds

1 tsp sea salt

½ tsp freshly ground black pepper

2 tbsp unsalted butter

2 tbsp honey

**Sesame seeds and honey give popcorn added crunch and sweetness. Store the popcorn in an airtight container – the popcorn stays fresh for a whole week, not that it ever lasts that long!**

1. Heat a heavy-based lidded frying pan over a medium heat. Add the oil and corn. Cover and return to the heat. Cook, shaking occasionally, until the corn start to pop. Turn up the heat and shake constantly.

2. Once the frantic popping slows to 2–3 seconds between pops, remove from the heat and pour into a large bowl. Remove any un-popped or partially popped kernels.

3. Return the pan to the heat. Add the sesame seeds and heat until the sesame seeds are lightly toasted. Add the sea salt, black pepper, butter and honey and melt gently. Pour over the popcorn and toss until evenly coated.

# LUNCHES

# SWEETCORN FRITTERS

SERVES 4

🔪 10 mins

🍳 15 mins

1 x 230g (8¾oz) can sweetcorn kernels, drained

3 spring onions, thinly sliced

½ tsp chilli flakes (optional)

Handful of coriander leaves, finely chopped

75g (3oz) plain flour

½ tsp baking powder

1 tsp salt

3 medium eggs, beaten

30ml (1floz) milk

Salt and freshly ground black pepper

Vegetable oil, for frying

Bacon, guacamole (see page 46) and soured cream, to serve

**A wonderful brunch or lunch dish or a perfect side dish to barbecued meats. The sweetcorn can be replaced with grated courgettes or carrots for equally delicious fritters.**

1. Place the drained sweetcorn in a medium-sized bowl and mix with the spring onions, chilli, if using, and coriander.

2. Sift the flour and baking powder and 1 teaspoon salt into a separate bowl.

3. Whisk together the eggs and milk until well combined.

4. Make a well in the centre of the flour bowl. Gradually pour the egg mixture into the well, whisking continuously, until the batter is smooth.

5. Stir in the corn mixture, season with salt and pepper and rest for 10 minutes.

6. Pour the oil into a large deep frying pan making sure the base of the pan is well covered. (CAUTION: hot oil can be dangerous. Do not leave unattended.) Heat the oil, add a tiny bit of batter, and if it immediately starts sizzling the oil is hot enough. Using 2 tablespoons of mixture per fritter, drop the mixture carefully into the pan. You should be able to cook 2–3 fritters at a time. Fry for 2–4 minutes on one side until a light brown, then turn over and cook for a further minute.

7. Transfer to a plate lined with kitchen paper. Repeat until all the batter is used. Serve with fried bacon, guacamole and soured cream.

# BAKED BEANS

🥄 15 mins

🍲 30 mins

3 tbsp vegetable oil

200g (7oz) smoked bacon lardons

1 onion, finely chopped

2 garlic cloves, grated

400ml (14floz) hot water

1 x 400g (14oz) can chopped tomatoes

2 tbsp tomato purée

50g (2oz) soft dark brown sugar

2 tbsp black treacle

1 tsp mustard powder

2 tbsp red wine vinegar

1 x 400g (14oz) can haricot beans, drained and rinsed

1 x 400g (14oz) can borlotti beans, drained and rinsed

Salt and freshly ground black pepper

Toasted bread and grated cheese, to serve

**The ultimate comfort food. It may not be as quick as your favourite 57 variety but it's definitely worth the extra effort. Delicious served with barbecued meat, spooned on to nachos, as well as on the humble buttered toast.**

1. In a large frying pan, heat the oil over a medium heat. Add the lardons and fry until crisp. Add the onion and garlic to the pan and cook until the onion is soft. Add the hot water to de-glaze the pan, scraping all the goodness from the bottom of the pan.

2. Add the chopped tomatoes, tomato purée, sugar, treacle, mustard powder and vinegar. Bring to the boil and simmer for 10 minutes. Add the beans. Reduce the heat and cook for a further 10 minutes, or until the mixture is piping hot and the sauce has thickened a little. Season to taste.

3. Serve with thick slices of toasted bread and a generous grating of cheese.

# FRENCH ONION SOUP

20g (¾oz) butter

1 tbsp oil

350g (12oz) onions, thinly sliced

½ tsp sugar

2 garlic cloves, sliced

3 sprigs thyme

1 tbsp flour

900ml (1½ pints) beef or vegetable stock

1 glass of white wine

1 small baguette, sliced

150g Gruyère or Emmenthal, grated

Chopped parsley, to serve

**This soup appears simple but the essential ingredient, when making this soup, is patience. Caramelising onions takes time, releasing the sweetness that makes this soup so deliciously rich.**

1. Melt the butter with the oil in a large, deep lidded heavy-based frying pan. Add the onions and cook with the lid on for 10 minutes until soft. Sprinkle in the sugar and cook for 20 minutes, stirring occasionally. Don't rush this stage, as the onions need to be soft and caramelised.

2. Add the garlic and thyme and cook for a further 5 minutes. Stir in the flour and cook for 3–4 minutes, then gradually pour in the stock and white wine. Partially cover with a lid and leave to simmer for a good 45 minutes.

3. Preheat the grill to high. Toast the baguette slices.

4. Place several thin slices of the toasted baguette onto the soup and cover with the cheese. Grill until the bread is toasted and the cheese has melted but not browned. Scatter with fresh chopped parsley and serve from the pan at the table remembering that the pan handle will be very hot.

# KIMCHI CHEESE TOASTIE

**SERVES 2**

5 mins

10 mins

4 thick slices bread, such as bloomer or sourdough

50g (2oz) mature Cheddar, grated

50g (2oz) Monterey Jack, grated

4–6 tbsp ready-prepared kimchi

2–3 tbsp butter, very soft

**Kimchi is a traditional fermented spicy Korean dish, which is made from vegetables including cabbage and a range of spices. This is a tasty makeover of the humble cheese and pickle sandwich.**

1. Generously pile half the bread slices with the cheese and top with a thick layer of the kimchi; press the other slices of bread on top to make the sandwiches.

2. Spread the outside of the bread with the butter. Heat a frying pan over a medium heat. Add the sandwiches and cook for 3–4 minutes until the bread on the underside turns golden and crisp. Flip the sandwiches over, squishing them down gently. Cook until the cheese starts to melt and both sides are golden and crisp. Cut the sandwiches in half and serve straight away.

# SPICY RED PEPPER SOUP

2 tbsp olive oil

3–4 red peppers, deseeded and roughly chopped

1 small onion, roughly chopped

2 garlic cloves, smashed

1 red chilli, sliced

700ml (1¼ pints) good-quality vegetable stock

2 large ripe tomatoes

75g (3oz) red split lentils

Salt and pepper

**Why buy sandwiches when you can enjoy home-made soup for lunch? If you are taking the soup to work, keep the croûtons separately and add after you have heated the soup.**

1. Heat a large deep frying pan and add the oil. Add the peppers and cook for about 10 minutes until lightly charred. Add the onion, garlic and chilli and cook for a further 10 minutes, or until the vegetables are soft and coloured. Season well.

2. Pour in the stock and add the tomatoes and lentils then bring to the boil. Reduce the heat down to a simmer and cook, covered, for 25 minutes until the peppers are tender. Blitz in a food processor until smooth, adding more stock or water if the consistency is too thick. Serve with croûtons (see below).

# PAN FRIED CROÛTONS

6–8 slices day-old white sandwich bread, crusts removed

4 tbsp unsalted butter

1 tbsp sunflower oil

Sea salt and freshly ground pepper

**Sprinkle these cubes into soups, or toss them into salads.**

1. Cut the bread into cubes. Heat a large non-stick pan over a medium heat. Melt half the butter and oil until bubbling. Add half the bread cubes; cook, tossing occasionally, until crisp and golden, about 2 minutes.

2. Drain on to a plate lined with kitchen paper. Repeat the process with remaining butter, oil and bread cubes. Season the croûtons with salt and pepper.

# AVOCADO *and* BLACK BEAN QUESADILLAS *with* PICKLED CUCUMBER

SERVES 4

🥄 15 mins

🍲 10 mins

## FOR THE QUESADILLAS:

1 large avocado, roughly chopped

200g (7oz) can black beans, drained and rinsed

125g (4½oz) pack mozzarella, drained and torn

100g (4oz) cherry tomatoes, quartered

3 spring onions, sliced

2 tbsp chopped coriander

Zest and juice of 1 lime

Olive oil, for frying

8 flour tortillas

125g (4½oz) Cheddar, grated

Salt and pepper

## FOR THE PICKLED CUCUMBER:

1 whole cucumber

1 tsp salt

50g (2oz) caster sugar

60ml (2½floz) cider vinegar

1 red chilli, halved

5cm (2in) fresh root ginger, peeled and grated

3 pieces stem ginger in syrup, sliced

**The Mexican version of the toasted sandwich, these crispy quesadillas are filled with gooey cheese, soft avocado and fresh juicy tomatoes, served with a sharp pickle. They make a perfect lunchtime meal. Chill any leftover cucumber pickle in an airtight jar.**

1. **For the cucumber pickle:** cut the cucumber into thin slices and put into a large bowl; sprinkle with salt and mix well. Leave the cucumber for 10 minutes to absorb the salt then rinse with cold water. Drain off the excess liquid in a colander. Return the cucumber to the large bowl. Combine the sugar, vinegar, chilli and the two types of ginger together. Add to the cucumber slices and mix well.

2. In a large bowl, mix together the avocado, black beans, mozzarella, cherry tomatoes, spring onions, coriander and the lime zest and juice. Season well.

3. Add a little olive oil to a large ovenproof frying pan. Put 1 tortilla in the pan and spoon one eighth of the mix over half the tortilla. Top with a handful of the Cheddar. Fold the tortillas over and press down with a spatula. Cook for 2 minutes, or until the base turns golden. Flip over and cook for a further couple of minutes.

4. Carefully remove the quesadilla from the pan and keep warm while you cook the remaining three. Serve the quesadillas with the pickled cucumber.

# TRIPLE DECKER CHEESE, CHICKEN *and* GRILLED PINEAPPLE SALSA QUESADILLAS

**SERVES 4**

🥄 10 mins

🍲 30 mins

**FOR THE SALSA LAYER:**

½ pineapple, peeled and cut into slices

1 tbsp olive oil

8 cherry tomatoes, quartered

¼ cucumber, finely diced

1 red onion, finely chopped

Pinch of sugar

1 red chilli, deseeded and finely chopped

Grated zest of 1 lime

2 tbsp fresh chopped mint

**FOR THE CHEESE AND CHICKEN LAYER:**

250g (9oz) Cheddar, grated

250g (9oz) cooked chicken, ripped into pieces

100g (4oz) sweetcorn

4 tbsp sour cream

2 tbsp olive oil

12 flour tortillas

Coriander, to serve

**This is the Tex Mex equivalent of the club sandwich. If time is short, use ready-made salsa. If you have time on your hands, make twice as much salsa and keep in the fridge to serve with tortilla chips or flat breads.**

1. **To make the salsa:** Heat a frying pan and rub the pineapple slices with a little oil. Cook in the hot frying pan until slightly charred. When cool enough to handle, dice.

2. Mix the pineapple, tomatoes, cucumber and red onion together. Add the sugar, half the chilli and the lime zest. Mix thoroughly and leave to stand for 30 minutes. Add the mint and toss gently.

3. **For the quesadillas:** Mix together the cheese, chicken, sweetcorn, remaining chilli and soured cream. Heat the frying pan over a low heat. Place one tortilla in the frying pan and spread over a quarter of the cheese mix. Top with another tortilla and spread with a spoonful of salsa. Top with a further tortilla, pressing down gently.

4. Cook the tortillas for 3–4 minutes, or until the cheese becomes gooey and the underneath is beginning to colour. When ready to flip, cover the frying pan with a plate and carefully invert the pan, slide the tortillas back into the pan and cook for further 3–4 minutes. Repeat with the other tortillas.

5. Serve sprinkled with coriander.

🔪 15 mins

🍲 15 mins

# SPRING VEGETABLE FRITTATA

300g (11oz) baby potatoes, such as Charlotte, halved if large

100g (4oz) peas, fresh or frozen

100g (4oz) broad beans, podded and shelled

6 large eggs

3 tbsp roughly chopped mint

1 tbsp olive oil

20g (¾oz) unsalted butter

1 small courgette, sliced

4 spring onions, thinly sliced

1 garlic clove, crushed

100g (4oz) feta, crumbled

Salt and pepper

**Such an adaptable dish – you can also use asparagus, broccoli and ham and top with goats' cheese or Cheddar. Perfect for a moveable feast, be it for work or a fun picnic.**

1. Place the potatoes in a deep 24cm (9½in) frying pan and cover with boiling water. Cook for 10–12 minutes, or until just tender. Drain and when cool enough to handle, slice thinly.

2. Tip the peas and broad beans into the frying pan and again cover with boiling water and cook for 2 minutes. Drain and refresh under cold water.

3. Beat the eggs in a medium bowl with the mint and season with salt and pepper.

4. Heat the oil and butter in the same frying pan. Add the courgette and cook for 1–2 minutes; then add the potatoes, spring onions and garlic, and cook for 3–4 minutes until beginning to brown. Stir in the peas and broad beans.

5. Preheat the grill. Pour the beaten egg over the vegetables and crumble over the feta. Cook over a gentle heat for 10–12 minutes until almost set. Transfer the pan to the grill and cook for 3–5 minutes until the top is golden and cooked through.

6. Place a plate or board over the top of the pan so that the frittata falls onto the plate. Slice into wedges and serve with a pea shoots, rocket and mint salad.

# PAN ROASTED POTATOES
## *with* HAM *and* SPRING ONIONS

SERVES 4

🥄 5 mins

🍲 20 mins

1 tbsp duck fat or olive oil

500g (1lb 2oz) small new potatoes, cleaned and halved if large

1 garlic clove, finely chopped

Juice of 1 lemon

6 spring onions

2 tbsp chopped parsley, tarragon and chives

250g (9oz) shredded ham hock

4 tbsp soured cream

Salt and pepper

**This recipe work best with those sweet new season potatoes. Don't peel, just clean gently. Also delicious with freshly podded peas and broad beans.**

1. Heat the duck fat or oil in a large frying pan over a medium-high heat. Add the potatoes in a single layer, cooking them in batches if necessary. Season and leave to cook for 5–6 minutes.

2. Add the garlic to the pan and continue to cook, turning occasionally, over a medium–high heat for 5 minutes, or until cooked through. Drain on kitchen paper and tip into a serving bowl. Pour over the lemon juice and season. Toss with the spring onions, herbs, ham and soured cream.

20 mins

30 mins

# SPICED CAULIFLOWER
# STEAKS *with* WALNUT PESTO

## FOR THE WALNUT PESTO:

125g (4½oz) walnuts

2 garlic cloves

Coarse sea salt and pepper

4 tbsp walnut oil

## FOR THE CAULIFLOWER STEAKS:

1 large head of cauliflower

50g (2oz) unsalted butter

1 tsp sweet paprika

1 tsp fresh thyme leaves

125g (4½oz) Stilton cheese

1 tbsp chopped parsley

**The humble cauliflower might not seem like the most exciting vegetable, but cut one into thick slabs and roast it with paprika, and you can transform it into quite the fine dish. These steaks can feel fancy enough for a dinner party, yet they're simple enough for an everyday lunch.**

1. Preheat the oven to 200°C, fan oven 180°C, Gas mark 6.

2. **Make the walnut pesto:** in a large, ovenproof frying pan, toast the walnuts over a medium heat until fragrant and slightly darkened, about 5 minutes. Do not turn your back when toasting nuts as they can burn really quickly. Transfer half the walnuts to a blender, add the garlic, salt, pepper and oil and whizz to combine.

3. Cut 'steaks' at least 2–3cm (1in) thick from the centre of the cauliflower (keep the end pieces and roast these as well).

4. Add the butter to the frying pan and place over a medium heat (or half the butter if you have to cook the cauliflower in batches). Once the butter starts to foam, add the cauliflower steaks, sprinkle with the sweet paprika and the thyme leaves. Spoon the butter over the cauliflower steaks. Cook gently for about 4 minutes until golden brown underneath, and then flip the steaks over. Cook for another 4 minutes until nearly cooked. Transfer to the oven for 10 minutes until the cauliflower is cooked through.

5. Roughly chop the remaining walnuts and crumble the cheese into small pieces. Serve the cauliflower sprinkled with the Stilton and alongside the walnut pesto. Sprinkle with parsley and remaining chopped walnuts.

# CAJUN CHICKEN *with* SEARED AVOCADOS

**SERVES 4**

🥄 20 mins

🍲 30 mins

4 chicken breasts with skin on

½ tsp Cajun seasoning

1 tbsp olive oil

2 small ripe avocados, peeled, halved and stoned

¼ tsp sugar

2 medium red onions, sliced into rings

1 red pepper, sliced

1 courgette, sliced

Juice of 1 lime

1 tbsp soy sauce

80ml (2½floz) soured cream

Salt and black pepper

Coriander and lime wedges, to serve

**No carbs needed with this dish, it is a meal in itself.**

1. Preheat the oven to 220°C, fan oven 200°C, Gas mark 7.

2. Season the chicken with salt and pepper and dust with the Cajun seasoning. Heat a large non-stick ovenproof frying pan over a medium-high heat. Add half the oil to the pan and add the chicken. Cook for 4 minutes then flip and cook for a further 2 minutes. Remove the chicken from the pan (it will finish cooking in the oven).

3. Wash the frying pan and return to a high heat. Sprinkle the avocados with the sugar. Add the avocados, cut side down, to the pan and cook for 2 minutes, or until charred. Remove the avocados from the pan.

4. Add the remaining oil to the pan and add the onions, red pepper and courgette and cook for 6 minutes until the onions and pepper are beginning to colour.

5. Stir in the lime juice and soy sauce. Nestle the chicken and avocados into the onion mixture. Place the pan in the oven and bake for 10 minutes, or until the chicken is cooked.

6. Remove the pan from the oven. Serve garnished with coriander and lime wedges.

# CHUNKY BUBBLE *and* SQUEAK TOPPED *with* SHREDDED HAM HOCK *and* FRIED EGG

Vegetable oil, for frying

½ medium onion, finely chopped

500g (1lb 2oz) Jersey Royals or other baby potatoes, cooked and crushed

125g (4½oz) shredded Savoy cabbage, blanched

150g (5oz) cooked carrots

3 tbsp chopped parsley

Lightly seasoned plain flour for coating

200g (7oz) shredded ham hock

4 eggs

Salt and pepper

**This could be served as a hearty brunch or a main course. A perfect way to use leftover vegetables from the Sunday lunch.**

1. Heat 1 tablespoon of oil in a large non-stick frying pan and add the onion. Cook over a low heat until softened but not coloured. Spoon the onion into a large bowl and combine with the potatoes, cabbage, carrots and parsley; mix well. Season with salt and pepper.

2. Shape the mixture by hand into four cakes and toss them in the flour to coat. Heat about 1cm (½in) of oil in the pan and fry the cakes for about 4 minutes on each side, or until slightly browned and holding together. Keep warm while you fry the eggs.

3. Increase the heat to medium-high, then break each egg into the pan and leave for about 30 seconds to begin to set. When the white looks almost set, turn the heat down low and using a metal spoon, baste the eggs all over with the fat in the pan. The yolk will cook lightly on top and become opaque. For a more well done egg, flip over using a palette knife or fish slice and cook for 5–10 seconds.

4. To serve, top each bubble and squeak cake with a pile of ham hock and a fried egg.

SERVES 2

🔪 10 mins

🍲 15 mins

# THAI COCONUT MUSSELS

1 kg (2lb 3oz) mussels, cleaned and debearded

4 spring onions, roughly chopped

2 lemon grass stems, roughly chopped

2cm (¾in) fresh ginger, peeled and roughly chopped

2 garlic cloves

2 green chillies, roughly chopped

1 large bunch of coriander

2 tbsp groundnut oil

400ml (14floz) coconut milk

1 tbsp fish sauce

Juice of 1 lime

1 x 250g (9oz) pouch steamed basmati rice

**If time is of the essence use ready-prepared Thai curry paste to make this, the most moreish of mussel dishes.**

1. Tap any open mussels and discard those that don't close. Put the spring onions, lemon grass, ginger, garlic, green chillies and coriander (reserving 1 tablespoon of leaves) into a food processor and whizz to a paste.

2. Heat the oil in a large, deep frying pan with a lid. Fry the paste for 2–3 minutes until the aroma is released. Add the coconut milk, fish sauce and lime juice and bring to a simmer. Add the mussels and rice and cover with the lid. Shake and steam for 3–4 minutes until all the mussels are open (discard any that stay closed). Serve the mussels scattered with the reserved coriander leaves.

# QUINOA *and* WARM HALLOUMI SALAD

**SERVES 2**

🥄 5 mins

🍲 10 mins

1 x 250g (9oz) pouch red and white quinoa

Juice of 1 lemon

2 tbsp extra virgin olive oil

2 tbsp olive oil

1 garlic clove, thinly sliced

3 baby courgettes, halved lengthways or 1 large courgette, sliced very thinly lengthways (a vegetable peeler is useful for this)

100g (4oz) roasted red pepper in oil, drained and sliced into 1cm (½in) strips

1 tbsp plain flour

150g (5oz) halloumi cheese, cut into 0.5cm (¼in) slices

Handful of pine nuts and rocket leaves, to serve

Salt and pepper

**Sometimes you are just too hungry to weigh, chop and wait – no need with this quick lunchtime salad. Roasted vegetables such as peppers, artichokes and olives in jars are great storecupboard ingredients to have.**

1. Heat a large frying pan over a medium heat and add the quinoa and a tablespoon of water and cook until the quinoa is hot. Mix the quinoa with the lemon juice and extra virgin olive oil and season to taste. Tip into a large serving bowl.

2. Heat 1 tablespoon of the oil in the frying pan, and gently cook the garlic for 2 minutes, making sure it does not burn. Add the courgettes and cook until they are just beginning to cook but still have some bite. Add to the quinoa. Add the red peppers and toss all the ingredients gently.

3. Dust the halloumi with the flour. Heat the remaining oil in the pan, and cook the halloumi on both sides until golden browned.

4. Serve the quinoa salad immediately, topped with the halloumi and sprinkled with the pine nuts and rocket leaves.

# OKONOMIYAKI JAPANESE PANCAKES

6 tbsp tomato ketchup

2 tbsp Worcestershire sauce

1 tbsp soy sauce

1 tbsp mirin

1 tbsp brown sugar

3 rashers streaky bacon

100g (4oz) plain flour

2 eggs, beaten

125ml (4½floz) chicken stock, cooled

250g (9oz) white or pointed cabbage, finely shredded

6 spring onions, shredded

2 tbsp vegetable oil

1 tbsp pickled sushi ginger, drained and chopped

1 tbsp sesame seeds

Salt and pepper

**Okonomi means 'how you want it' and an okonomiyaki is one of the world's most adaptable dishes. The shredded or chopped cabbage is the base but, after that, it is down to you – prawns, shredded duck or chicken all work well.**

1. Mix together the tomato ketchup, Worcestershire sauce, soy sauce, mirin and sugar to make a sauce.

2. Heat a small 20cm (8in) non-stick frying pan, add the bacon and cook over a medium-high heat for a few minutes until cooked through. Remove the bacon from the pan and set aside. Once cool, cut into large pieces.

3. Put the plain flour into a large bowl. Whisk in the eggs and the cooled chicken stock to make a batter. Season.

4. Stir in the cabbage and half the spring onions. Heat half the oil in a non-stick frying pan. Tip in half the batter mix and press down with a spatula so it fills the pan. Add the bacon.

5. Cook over a medium heat until the underside is golden and cooked through and it has set enough to turn. Slide it on to a plate, uncooked-side up. Put the frying pan over the plate and use the plate to turn the pancake, uncooked-side down, back into the pan. Keep cooking, pressing down with a spatula until the inside is cooked and piping hot. Keep warm while cooking the other pancake with the remaining batter and oil.

6. Serve the pancakes drizzled with the sauce and sprinkled with the ginger, sesame seeds and remaining spring onions.

# CHICKPEA PANCAKES *topped with* CHICKPEA *and* TOMATO *and* NUTTY YOGHURT

SERVES 2

🥄 30 mins

🍲 15 mins

## FOR THE PANCAKE BATTER:

1 x 400g (14oz) can chickpeas, drained and rinsed

2 large eggs

3 tbsp milk

4 tbsp plain flour

1 tsp baking powder

4 spring onions, chopped

2 tsp harissa

Oil, for frying

## FOR THE CHICKPEA AND TOMATO TOPPING:

2 tbsp olive oil

1 x 400g (14oz) can chickpeas, drained and rinsed

10 cherry tomatoes, halved

15 kalamata olives, pitted and halved

1 red onion, thinly sliced

1 tsp cumin seeds

2 tbsp preserved lemon, finely chopped

## FOR THE TOASTED NUTTY YOGHURT:

2 tbsp pine nuts

100g (4oz) walnut halves

1 garlic clove

150g (5oz) Greek yoghurt

3 tbsp extra virgin olive oil

1 tsp dried dill

½ tsp salt

Chopped mint, to serve

**A pancake fritter hybrid, this recipe makes the most of canned chickpeas – a storecupboard staple. Toasted as a snack, essential for houmous, delicious in salads and of course as a basis for dhal.**

1. **For the toasted nutty yoghurt**: heat a dry frying pan and add the pine nuts and walnuts. Cook, agitating the pan every now and again until the nuts are nicely toasted. Don't turn your back on the pan as the nuts can burn easily. Cool for 10 minutes and place the toasted nuts into the bowl of a food processor. Add the garlic and pulse until ground. You could also simply chop these by hand for a chunkier texture. Transfer the nut and garlic mixture to a large bowl. Fold in the yoghurt, olive oil, dill and salt. Chill until ready to use.

2. **For the pancake batter**: place half the chickpeas in a food processor and whizz for 30 seconds. Add the eggs, milk, flour and baking powder. Whizz the mixture on high speed until smooth. Scrape down the sides and whizz again until completely smooth. Fold in the reserved whole chickpeas, spring onions and harissa.

3. Heat a heavy-based frying pan and when hot add 1 tablespoon oil. Spoon 3 tablespoons batter into the pan. Cook until bubbles rise to the top and the edges become golden brown. Flip and cook on the other side until done. Keep making pancakes until you use all the batter. Keep warm.

4. **To make the chickpea topping**: put the olive oil in a large frying pan and add the chickpeas. Cook, swirling the pan until the chickpeas start to take on colour. Add the tomatoes, olives, red onion, cumin seeds and preserved lemon. Cook for about 15 minutes, or until the onions soften and the chickpeas become golden and toasty.

5. To serve, arrange some pancakes on a plate and serve with the chickpea topping and a dollop of yogurt, a scattering of fresh mint, and a final drizzle of olive oil.

# POTATO *and* HORSERADISH RÖSTI *topped with* SMOKED MACKEREL *and* BEETROOT

## FOR THE RÖSTI:

500g (1lb 2oz) waxy potatoes such as Charlotte, grated

4 spring onions, finely chopped

1 tsp creamed horseradish

1 tbsp butter, melted

2 tbsp oil

Salt and pepper

## FOR THE TOPPING:

2 smoked mackerel fillets, skinned

2 tbsp of mayonnaise

1 punnet cress

1 cooked beetroot, very thinly sliced

Lemon wedges, to serve

**Take time to dry the potatoes well before starting the rösti, as this is what gives the rösti its crisp crust. Serve with poached eggs, fried eggs, bacon or it's delicious with smoked salmon and crème fraîche.**

1. Put the grated potato in a clean tea towel or muslin and squeeze out as much moisture as you can. Unfold the tea towel, mix the potatoes and repeat the process. You need to have the potatoes as dry as possible and this prevents the rösti from being soggy. Tip the potatoes into a bowl with the spring onions, horseradish and half the butter. Season well.

2. Heat the remaining butter and half the oil in a 20cm (8in) frying pan over a medium heat until foaming. Add the potato mix and press the mixture into the pan using the back of a spoon to shape into a flat cake. Allow to cook for a couple of minutes, and gently shake the pan to loosen the potato.

3. Continue to cook over a low heat for about 10 minutes until golden and crisp, then place a plate on top of the pan and invert it so the cake sits cooked-side up on the plate.

4. Add the rest of the oil to the pan and, when hot, slide the potato cake back into the pan the other way up. Cook for another 10 minutes.

5. Break the smoked mackerel into bite-sized pieces and add to a bowl with the mayonnaise and cress.

6. Serve the rösti topped with the beetroot and smoked mackerel and lemon wedges.

# FLATBREADS

250g (9oz) self-raising flour, plus extra for dusting

½ tsp baking powder

250g (9oz) Greek yoghurt

Pinch of salt

1 tbsp olive oil

**These incredibly versatile breads are the ideal partner to everything from houmous to curries; they are perfect to mop up the juices of a tagine.**

1. Put the flour, baking powder and yoghurt into a large bowl with a generous pinch of salt. Mix with a wooden spoon to form a rough dough. Tip out on to a lightly floured surface and knead until smooth. Divide into four equal portions, then roll or pat until each is around 1cm (½in) thick. Brush with a little oil.

2. Heat a heavy-based pan over a medium heat. Cook the flatbreads for 2–3 minutes on each side until slightly puffed and golden. Repeat with the remaining dough.

3. You need to stack the breads in a clean towel and let them steam together for a moment or two so they can fully soften to their final, perfect texture.

## FLAVOURED FLATBREADS

**THYME FLATBREADS:**
Add 1 tablespoon of thyme leaves to the flour mix. Continue as above.

**SESAME SEED FLATBREADS:**
Add 2 tablespoons of black sesame seeds to the flour mix. Continue as above.

**HERB BUTTER FLATBREADS:**

100g (4oz) unsalted butter

Handful of fresh flatleaf parsley, chopped

Juice of ½ lemon

Sea salt

Once the flatbreads are cooked, melt the butter in a frying pan over a low heat. Stir in the parsley, lemon juice and a good pinch of salt. Drizzle the butter over the flatbreads just before serving.

**ZA'ATAR OIL FLATBREADS:**

3 tbsp olive oil

1 tbsp za'atar

Cook the flatbreads as above. When still hot brush with the olive oil and sprinkle with the za'atar.

# LEBANESE LAMB TOPPED FLATBREADS

1 tbsp vegetable oil

1 red onion, sliced

1 garlic clove, chopped

1 tsp ground coriander

1 tsp ground cumin

1 tbsp baharat spice blend

1 tbsp dried mint

500g (1lb 2oz) British lamb mince

1 tbsp pomegranate molasses

75g (3oz) apricots, chopped

300ml (10floz) chicken stock

1 quantity flatbread dough (see opposite)

Salt and pepper

Greek yoghurt, pine nuts, pomegranate seeds and fresh mint, to serve

**Baharat spice is a blend of spices usually including black pepper, coriander, paprika, cardamom, nutmeg, cumin, cloves, paprika and cinnamon. Use baharat as a dry rub for grilled meat or mix it with butter for basting chicken. Alternatively, you can mix it with some olive oil and use it as a marinade before barbecuing.**

1. Heat the oil in a large frying pan; add the onion, garlic, spices and dried mint. Cook for 2 minutes before stirring in the lamb mince. Cook over a high heat, turning often and breaking up the mince clumps with a wooden spoon, until browned all over.

2. Add the pomegranate molasses, apricots and chicken stock and bring to the boil. Reduce the heat and simmer for 20 minutes, or until the mince is tender and the stock has nearly all evaporated. Taste and season with salt and pepper.

3. Cook the flatbreads (see opposite) and serve with the lamb, topped with the yoghurt, pine nuts, pomegranate seeds and mint.

# THREE CHEESE
# MACARONI CHEESE

**SERVES 4**

🥄 15 mins

🍲 20 mins

250g (9oz) macaroni pasta

100g (4oz) mature Cheddar, grated

50g (2oz) Gruyère cheese, grated

25g (1oz) Parmesan, finely grated

600ml (1 pint) milk

40g (1½oz) plain flour

40g (1½oz) butter

Pinch of mustard powder

¼ tsp grated nutmeg

100g (4oz) stale bread

Salt and freshly milled black pepper

**One pan, one plastic whisk, one wooden spoon, four plates and four forks... serve!**

1. Preheat the oven to 220°C, fan oven 200°C, Gas mark 7.

2. Tip the macaroni into a large deep frying pan and cover in boiling water. Stir and cook for 7–9 minutes, or until just al dente. Drain the macaroni and set aside while making the sauce.

3. **For the sauce:** put all three cheeses (using only half the Cheddar), milk, flour, butter and mustard powder into the deep frying pan. Heat over a medium heat, bring to a gentle simmer for about 10 minutes whisking continually until you have a smooth, glossy sauce. Season with salt and pepper and grated nutmeg.

4. Add the cooked macaroni and stir well. Tear the bread into large chunks and scatter over the macaroni. Sprinkle with the remaining cheese.

5. Bake in the oven for about 15–20 minutes, or until the top is bubbling and the bread is crunchy.

🥄 1½ hours

🍲 10 mins

# CHARGRILLED TOPPED PAN BAKED PIZZA

## FOR THE DOUGH:

250g (9oz) strong white bread flour

½ x 7g sachet fast action yeast

½ tsp sea salt

150ml (5floz) warm water

## FOR THE TOPPING:

6 tbsp chargrilled peppers, artichokes and courgettes in oil, drained

6 slices prosciutto or ham

1 x 125g (4½oz) ball mozzarella, torn

Olive oil, for drizzling

Handful of rocket

**Making the dough may take a bit of time and waiting but the cooking of these pizzas is very quick. Top with your favourite topping for a family favourite meal.**

1. **To make the pizza dough**: put the flour in a large mixing bowl with the yeast and salt. Make a well in the centre and pour in most of the warm water. Mix to a soft dough, drawing in the flour from the sides with your hand. If the dough is too dry, add a little more warm water.

2. Knead the dough by hand on a well-floured work surface for 10 minutes. Alternatively, do this in a food mixer fitted with a dough hook for 5 minutes. It should feel smooth, silky and elastic.

3. Place in a large lightly oiled bowl and cover with cling film or a damp cloth. Leave in a warm place for 1 hour until it rises and doubles in size. Knock down the dough with your fist. Knead it lightly on a floured surface.

4. Divide the dough into two pieces and press them flat on to a floured work surface. Roll them out to about 0.5cm (¼in) thick.

5. Preheat the grill to its absolute highest setting.

6. Heat a large 24cm (9½in) non-stick ovenproof frying pan until very hot. Lay one of the pizza bases in the dry frying pan. Reduce the heat to low.

7. Scatter the pizza base with half the vegetables, scrunched up prosciutto slices and mozzarella. Drizzle with olive oil.

8. Cook the pizza for about 2–4 minutes until the pizza has browned underneath. Transfer the frying pan to the grill. Cook for a further 1–2 minutes or until the crust and topping is a golden brown. Serve topped with a handful of rocket. Repeat with the other pizza base.

# TWO INGREDIENTS PIZZA DOUGH:

## GORGONZOLA *and* CARAMELISED ONION PIZZA

SERVES 2

➥ 5 mins

🍲 20 mins

1 tbsp oil

1 tbsp butter

2 red onions, cut into eighths

1 tbsp crème fraîche

75g (3oz) Gorgonzola or dolcelatte

155g (5¼oz) self-raising flour

185g (6½oz) Greek yoghurt

50g (2oz) walnuts, roughly chopped

A few sage leaves, to garnish

**This pizza dough is nothing short of magic – made with just two ingredients. All you need to do is load it up with your favourite pizza toppings.**

1. Heat the oil and butter in a large 24cm (9½in) non-stick frying pan. Add the onion and cook for 20 minutes, or until the onions are soft and caramelised. Spoon into a bowl and wipe the frying pan clean.

2. Mix together the crème fraîche and the blue cheese in a small bowl. Do not overmix; leave some of the cheese lumps remaining.

3. **For the dough**: put the flour and yoghurt into a large bowl and, using clean hands, bring the mixture together to form a dough. Dust a clean surface with flour, turn the dough out and lightly knead until smooth. Cut in half and use a rolling pin to roll out into a rough circle, about 24cm (9½in) diameter. Don't worry too much about the shape. Repeat with the other half.

4. Preheat the grill to its absolute highest setting.

5. Heat the frying pan until very hot. Lay one of the pizza bases in the dry frying pan. Reduce the heat to low.

6. Spread the pizza base with half of the cheese mix. Sprinkle over the caramelised onion, followed by half the walnuts.

7. Cook the pizza for about 3–4 minutes until it has browned underneath. Place the frying pan on the highest shelf, under the grill. Cook for a further 1–2 minutes, or until the crust and topping is a golden brown. Cut each pizza into wedges and sprinkle with a few sage leaves. Repeat with the other pizza base.

# ALTERNATIVE TOPPINGS

## CHICKEN AND PESTO

3 tbsp basil pesto

1 cooked chicken breast

2 tbsp kalamata olives

4 tbsp Parmesan cheese, grated

6 basil leaves

2 tbsp toasted pine nuts

1. Heat a large 24cm (9½in) non-stick ovenproof frying pan until very hot. Lay one of the pizza bases in the dry frying pan and reduce the heat to low.

2. Spread 1½ tablespoons of the pesto onto the prepared pizza base followed by half the chicken, olives and cheese.

3. Cook the pizza for about 2–4 minutes until it has browned underneath. Transfer the frying pan under the grill. Cook for a further 1–2 minutes or until the crust and topping is a golden brown. Serve topped with the basil leaves and pine nuts. Repeat with the other pizza base.

## CLASSIC MARGHERITA

4 tbsp passata

Drizzle of extra virgin olive oil

½ ball of mozzarella, torn into medium pieces

Handful of basil leaves

1. Spread 2 tablespoons of the passata onto each pizza. Drizzle with a little olive oil and top with the mozzarella.

2. Heat a large 24cm (9½in) non-stick ovenproof frying pan until very hot. Lay one of the pizza bases in the dry frying pan and reduce the heat to low.

3. Cook the pizza for about 2–4 minutes until it has pizza has browned underneath. Transfer the frying pan under the grill. Cook for a further 1–2 minutes or until the crust and topping is a golden brown. Serve topped with the basil leaves. Repeat with the other pizza base.

## BRIE AND FIG

50g Brie

2 slices smoked ham, chopped

2 fresh figs, quartered

Drizzle of balsamic vinegar and extra virgin olive oil

1. Heat a large 24cm (9½in) non-stick ovenproof frying pan until very hot. Lay one of the pizza bases in the dry frying pan and reduce the heat to low.

2. Cook the pizza for about 2–4 minutes until it has browned underneath. Flip over and cook for a further 2 minutes.

3. Slide the cooked base onto a plate and spread 25g Brie over it. Top with half the ham, figs and drizzle with the balsamic and olive oil. Repeat with the other pizza base.

# PAN FRIED GNOCCHI
*with* TOMATOES, PURPLE SPROUTING BROCCOLI *and* HAZELNUTS

SERVES 2

🥄 15 mins

🍲 15 mins

25g (1oz) blanched hazelnuts

3 tbsp olive oil

1 tbsp butter

500g (1lb 2oz) potato gnocchi

200g (7oz) purple sprouting broccoli, cut into 3cm (1¼in) pieces

2 garlic cloves, thinly sliced

1 shallot, thinly sliced

250g (9oz) mixed baby tomatoes, halved

Pinch of chilli flakes

Zest of 1 lemon

50g (2oz) Parmesan cheese, coarsely grated

**Fresh and simple, with the added nutty dimension of the roasted hazelnuts. Why not toast a whole bag of hazelnuts and keep the rest to add to your morning porridge or a salad?**

1. Heat a large frying pan over a medium heat, and add the hazelnuts. Agitate the pan frequently until the nuts turn a golden brown and there is a delicious nutty toasted aroma. Do not turn your back on these or they will burn in an instant. Remove the hazelnuts from pan, and when cool enough, roughly chop. Wipe the pan with kitchen paper.

2. Heat 1 tablespoon of the oil and butter in a large frying pan. Add the gnocchi and cook over a medium heat for 5 minutes, tossing regularly. Remove from the pan ready to use later.

3. Add another tablespoon of oil to the frying pan and add the broccoli; cook for 5 minutes until the broccoli is slightly charred. Remove using a slotted spoon ready to use later.

4. Return the frying pan to the heat and fry the garlic and shallot gently in the remaining tablespoon of oil for about 2 minutes, or until golden. Add the tomatoes and chilli flakes and cook for 2 minutes. Return the gnocchi and broccoli to the pan and gently toss together. Serve sprinkled with the hazelnuts, lemon zest and Parmesan.

# BLUE CHEESE GNOCCHI
*with* BACON *and* SPINACH

**SERVES 2**

🥄 5 mins

🍳 15 mins

1 tbsp olive oil

1 tbsp butter

500g (1lb 2oz) gnocchi

2 rashers bacon, finely chopped

50g (2oz) Danish Blue cheese or similar blue cheese

2 tbsp milk

50g (2oz) baby spinach leaves, trimmed and chopped

**Gnocchi is a great storecupboard item. If you fancy roast potatoes but don't fancy peeling potatoes – just pan fry gnocchi in oil until they are golden and crispy.**

1. Heat the oil and butter in a 24cm (9½in) non-stick frying pan. Add the gnocchi and cook over a medium heat for 5 minutes, tossing regularly. Remove from the pan to use later. Add the bacon to the pan and cook until the bacon is beginning to colour.

2. Mash the cheese into the milk in a small bowl.

3. Add the spinach and cooked gnocchi to the pan and stir for 2–3 minutes until the spinach is wilted. Add the mashed cheese and toss until melted into a sauce. Serve immediately.

# BEEF KEEMA *with* SPICY MANGO CHUTNEY

**FOR THE KEEMA:**

1 tbsp oil

1 large onion, chopped

1 carrot, finely diced

2 garlic cloves, crushed

4cm (2in) piece ginger, grated

2 green chillies, thinly sliced

500g (1lb 2oz) beef mince

1 tbsp garam masala

2 tsp turmeric

2 tomatoes, chopped

2 tbsp tomato purée

½ stick cinnamon

3 cloves

200g (7oz) frozen peas

1 small bunch of coriander, chopped

**FOR THE CHUTNEY:**

2 tsp vegetable oil

2–5 dried red chillies, to taste

1 tsp cumin seeds

1 tsp fennel seeds

180ml (6floz) white wine vinegar

1–2 tbsp brown sugar

160ml (5½floz) water

2 large ripe mangoes, peeled, stoned and cut into pieces

Salt and pepper

**Don't be put off by the number of ingredients, it's actually a really simple recipe. You can always serve with shop-bought mango chutney.**

1. **For the chutney:** heat the oil in a non-stick frying pan and add the whole chillies, cumin seeds and fennel seeds. Once the cumin is aromatic and the chillies are darker, add the vinegar, sugar, water and a little salt and pepper. Simmer for 6–7 minutes. Add the mango and cook for 6–7 minutes, or until the mango is soft and easy to mash. Spoon the chutney into a bowl and mash half the mango pieces into the chutney and mix well. It should be thick, but not jammy.

2. **For the keema:** heat the oil in a large ovenproof frying pan and cook the onions until softened, then add the carrot, garlic, ginger and sliced chillies. Cook for about 2 minutes, until fragrant. Add the mince and cook until it begins to brown, using a fork to break up any lumps. When it is browned, add the garam masala and turmeric and fry for 1 minute.

3. Add the tomatoes and tomato purée. Bring to a simmer, season with salt and black pepper, add the cinnamon and cloves and stir well. Cover and simmer for at least 40 minutes. At the end of the cooking time, add the frozen peas and cook for 5 minutes more.

4. Sprinkle the keema with coriander and serve with rice or naan and the chutney.

# ONE PAN LEMON GARLIC PASTA

SERVES 2

5 mins

10 mins

50g (2oz) butter

2 garlic cloves, finely chopped

500ml (15½floz) water

200g (7oz) linguine, snapped in half

Zest and juice of 1 lemon

50g (2oz) black pepper cream cheese

1 tbsp fresh tarragon or 1 tsp dried tarragon

Handful of rocket

**This is a wonderfully fresh and simple lunchtime dish. When zesting a lemon try and buy the unwaxed version or better still buy Amalfi lemons – the queen of lemons.**

1. Heat half the butter in a large frying pan with a lid over medium heat. Add the garlic and cook for about 30 seconds, being careful not to burn.

2. Add the water, linguine, remaining butter, lemon zest and juice to the pan. Bring to the boil, stirring with tongs to make sure the pasta is separated and does not stick to the bottom of the pan. Cook for about 9 minutes, or until the pasta is cooked and the liquid has nearly evaporated to create a sauce. Add the cream cheese and tarragon and toss until the cheese has melted into the sauce.

3. Serve garnished with a handful of rocket.

# DINNERS

# BUTTERNUT SQUASH
## *and* SWEET POTATO CURRY

**SERVES 4**

🥄 10 mins

🍲 40–50 mins

3 tbsp vegetable oil

50g (2oz) ready-made red Thai curry paste from a jar

1 tbsp palm sugar or brown sugar

2 x 350g (12oz) bags prepared butternut and sweet potato

1 x 400ml (14floz) can coconut milk

90ml (2¾floz) coconut cream

½ tbsp fish sauce

2cm (1in) piece ginger, peeled and finely shredded

2 sticks lemon grass, bruised

1 tbsp lime pickle from a jar

Coriander and naan bread, to serve

**Adding lime pickle to this curry is a delicious twist. If you are uncertain of the heat add half a tablespoon first and gradually add more until you get the perfect spicy heat.**

1. Heat the oil in a large deep frying pan over a medium heat and fry the curry paste for 2 minutes until fragrant. Add the palm sugar and cook for 4–5 minutes until the mixture is sticky.

2. Stir in the squash and sweet potato and cook for 2–3 minutes.

3. Add the coconut milk, coconut cream, fish sauce, ginger and lemon grass and bring to the boil. Reduce the heat to simmer for 20–30 minutes, or until the squash and potatoes are tender but not mushy. Add the lime pickle and cook for 2–3 minutes. Check the balance of flavours, adapting with extra pickle or fish sauce. Serve with lots of coriander and naan breads.

# BUTTERNUT *and* POMEGRANATE PILAF *topped with* CRISPY SHALLOTS *and* GARLIC

FOR THE CRISPY SHALLOTS
AND GARLIC:

**Vegetable oil, for frying**

**3 small shallots, thinly sliced
into rings**

**2 garlic cloves, thinly sliced**

**Salt**

*Continued opposite*

**The pomegranate seeds give the dish a pop of juicy freshness. Don't feel you have to use all the seeds from one pomegranate; keep in the fridge and use the seeds to top your morning yoghurt, porridge or your lunchtime salad.**

1. **For the crispy shallots and garlic**: heat 1cm (½in) vegetable oil in a heavy-based frying pan over a medium heat until shimmering. Working in three batches, add the shallots and garlic and cook until golden brown, about 2 minutes. Transfer to a kitchen paper-lined plate to drain and season with salt. Pour the oil away leaving about a tablespoon in the frying pan.

## FOR THE PILAF:

1 tbsp vegetable oil

1 onion, chopped

1 x 350g (12oz) bag prepared butternut squash

¾ tsp ground cinnamon

¼ tsp ground cardamom

½ tsp whole black peppercorns

½ tsp chilli flakes

10 cloves

225g (8oz) basmati rice

2½cm (1in) piece ginger, peeled and finely grated

1 garlic clove, crushed

75g (3oz) dried soft apricots, roughly chopped

50g (2oz) sultanas

600ml (1 pint) vegetable stock

50g (2oz) flaked pistachios, toasted

Handful of pomegranate seeds

Handful of chopped fresh parsley

2. **For the pilaf:** heat the oil in the pan, add the onion and butternut squash, and cook gently for about 7 minutes, or until the onion is beginning to soften and the squash is starting to take on colour.

3. Add the spices and rice and stir until everything is coated in the spices. Add the ginger and garlic and cook for 30 seconds more. Add the apricots and sultanas. Pour in the stock, stir and cover with a lid. Keep covered and cook for 20 minutes, shaking the pan every now and again.

4. Once the rice is tender and the stock has been absorbed, sprinkle with the pistachios and pomegranate seeds. Serve topped with crispy fried shallots and chopped parsley.

# LENTIL *and* SWEET POTATO DHAL *with* MINTY YOGHURT

SERVES 4

⟶ 10 mins

🍲 25 mins

## FOR THE LENTIL AND SWEET POTATO DHAL:

1 tbsp coconut oil

1 onion, thinly sliced

3 garlic cloves, finely chopped

2cm (1in) piece fresh ginger, peeled and cut into thin strips

½ long red chilli, deseeded and thinly sliced

1 tsp ground turmeric

1 tsp ground coriander

1 tsp ground cumin

½ cayenne pepper

1 large sweet potato, peeled and cut into 2cm (1in) chunks

250g (9oz) red lentils, rinsed

700ml (1¼pt) vegetable stock

3 tomatoes, chopped

Salt and freshly ground black pepper

Coriander leaves, to serve

## FOR THE MINTY YOGHURT:

150g (5oz) thick Greek yoghurt

2 spring onions, finely chopped

2 tbsp chopped mint leaves

**A vegetarian dish that will warm you up on a cold winter's night; mind you equally delicious in the height of summer!**

1. **For the minty yoghurt**: combine the yoghurt, spring onion and mint. Chill until ready to use.

2. **For the lentil and sweet potato dahl**: heat the oil in a large frying pan with a tight-fitting lid. Add the onion and cook for about 10 minutes, or until soft and starting to colour. Add the garlic, ginger and chilli and cook for a further minute. Add the spices and cook for a couple of minutes, or until the aroma is released. Add a tablespoon of water just to loosen the mixture.

3. Stir in the sweet potato and coat in spice mix. Add the lentils and stock and bring to the boil. Reduce the heat, cover and cook for 10 minutes. Add the tomatoes, cover and cook for a further 5 minutes, or until the lentils are tender. If the dhal is too soupy, increase the heat and cook a little longer; if it's too thick, add a dash of water.

4. Serve the dhal with the minted yoghurt and sprinkled with fresh coriander.

5 mins

16 mins

# SPANISH PRAWNS *and* RICE

1 tbsp oil

75g (3oz) chorizo, sliced

1 onion, sliced

2 red peppers, deseeded
and sliced

2 garlic cloves, crushed

2 tsp smoked paprika

250g (9oz) easy-cook
basmati rice

1 x 400g (14oz) can cherry
tomatoes

250ml (9floz) vegetable stock

250ml (9floz) white wine

200g (7oz) raw, peeled
prawns, defrosted if frozen

100g (4oz) peas

2 tbsp fresh chopped parsley

**There are a few items you should always have in your larder
and chorizo is one of them. If you have chorizo, a bag of frozen
prawns and peas – you have dinner!**

1. Heat the oil in a non-stick frying pan with a lid. Add the chorizo
   and cook for 2 minutes just to release the oil. Add the onion,
   peppers and garlic and cook over a high heat for 5 minutes. Stir in
   the paprika, rice, tomatoes, stock and wine. Cover and then cook
   over a medium heat for 12 minutes.

2. Remove the lid and stir in the prawns and peas. Cook for 3–4
   minutes, or until the prawns are pink and cooked and the rice is
   tender. Fluff with a fork before serving sprinkled with parsley.

# KALE, CABBAGE *and* COCONUT THORAN

**SERVES 4**

🥄 15 mins

🍲 20 mins

2 tbsp coconut oil

1 tsp black mustard seeds

4 curry leaves

1 tsp cumin seeds

1 tbsp finely grated fresh ginger

½ tsp ground turmeric

1 onion, thinly sliced

2 garlic cloves, crushed

1 green chilli, thinly sliced

90g (3¾oz) prepared fresh coconut chunks, very finely chopped

250g (9oz) kale, shredded

250g (9oz) spring cabbage, shredded

Juice of ½ lemon

Salt and pepper

**Thoran is a dry vegetable curry from Kerala made from whatever fresh vegetables are around – green beans, spinach or courgettes. Serve on its own or with rice and naan.**

1. Heat the coconut oil in a heavy-based frying pan over a medium heat, and, when hot, add the mustard seeds followed by the curry leaves and cumin seeds. Stir for about 30 seconds, add the ginger and turmeric, salt and black pepper and fry for 30 seconds. When the seeds crackle in the heat, add the sliced onion. Cook for about 10 minutes until soft and starting to caramelise, then add the garlic and green chilli and stir-fry for a couple of minutes.

2. Add the coconut, kale and cabbage and keep stirring for around 4–6 minutes, or until the kale and cabbage is wilted and tender. Squeeze over the lemon juice and serve.

# SPANISH SEAFOOD PAELLA

Large pinch of saffron strands

600ml (1 pint) vegetable or chicken stock

3 tbsp olive oil

100g (4oz) chorizo, roughly chopped

500g (1lb 2oz) boneless, skinless chicken thighs, cut into large chunks

1 onion, finely chopped

3 garlic cloves, finely chopped

2 tsp paprika

250g (9oz) Spanish paella rice

4 medium tomatoes, roughly chopped

200g (7oz) jumbo tiger prawns, fresh or defrosted

200g (7oz) live mussels, cleaned and debearded

75g (3oz) frozen peas

150g (5oz) squid rings

Small handful of flat-leaf parsley

Lemon wedges, to serve

Salt and pepper

**Many of us have had those wonderful paellas on holiday, loaded with fresh local seafood and often a bit of the local sand! Make the version at home with the best selection of fresh fish you can source.**

1. Soak the saffron strands in the stock.

2. Heat 1 tablespoon of the oil in a large, deep pan with a lid. Add the chorizo and cook for 5 minutes or until the chorizo has released the red oil. Remove the chorizo with a slotted spoon and drain on kitchen paper.

3. Add the chicken to the pan and cook over a high heat for about 8 minutes, or until the meat is starting to turn golden around the edges. Transfer the chicken to a bowl and set aside to use later.

4. Pour another tablespoon of oil into the pan, add the onion and garlic and stir-fry for 4–5 minutes, until the onion is softened and just starting to colour. Stir in the paprika with the remaining tablespoon of oil and cook, stirring, for a further 1–2 minutes. All the fried bits on the bottom of the pan will add to the flavour of the paella.

5. With the heat still quite high, stir in the rice and coat in the oil, pour in the saffron stock plus 450ml (15floz) boiling water. Scrape up all the bits from the bottom of the pan. Return the chicken to the pan and add the chopped tomatoes. Cook uncovered over a medium heat for 10 minutes, shaking the pan very occasionally. Add the prawns and live mussels, pushing them well into the rice. Cook for 5 minutes then scatter in the peas and chorizo over the top.

6. Cook for a further 5 minutes, or until the rice is just cooked and most of the liquid in the pan has been absorbed. Add the squid and cook for a further 3 minutes, or until the squid is just cooked but not rubbery. (Remove any mussels that may not have opened.) Towards the end of the cooking, stop shaking the pan so a crispy layer of toasted rice forms on the bottom, known as *soccarat* (the most delicious bit of all).

7. Take the pan off the heat before the rice is totally cooked through and cover the pan in foil, leaving it to cook under its own steam for 5–10 minutes.

8. Season to taste with salt and pepper and serve scattered with the parsley and a pile of lemon wedges.

# APPLE, CHICKEN *and* SWEET POTATO PAN FRY

3 tbsp olive oil

2 garlic cloves, crushed

1 tbsp chopped fresh rosemary

1 tsp ground cinnamon

6 boneless, skinless chicken thighs

4 slices thick-cut bacon, chopped

8 shallots, peeled

200g (7oz) Brussels sprouts, trimmed and halved

1 medium sweet potato, peeled and cut into cubes

2 Granny Smith or other firm apples, peeled, cored and cut into wedges

100ml (3½floz) cider or apple juice

125ml (4½floz) chicken stock

150ml (5floz) crème fraîche

Salt and black pepper

**Chicken and apple is such a warming, delicious combination. The other vegetables in this recipe are more adaptable – swap onions or leeks for the shallots, kale or cabbage for the sprouts and butternut squash for the sweet potatoes.**

1. Mix together 2 tablepoons of the olive oil, the garlic, rosemary and cinnamon. Season with salt and pepper and pour into a resealable plastic bag. Add the chicken thighs; seal the bag shake to coat the chicken. Chill until ready to use.

2. Heat the remaining oil in a large, non-stick frying pan over a medium-high heat. Add the bacon and shallots and cook for about 4 minutes, then add the sprouts and sweet potato. Cook until the bacon is crispy and the shallots are soft and beginning to take on colour. Add the apples and cook for 2–3 minutes. Remove from the pan and set aside until later.

3. Add the chicken and marinade to the pan and cook for about 7–9 minutes, or until the chicken is lightly browned and cooked through. Return the bacon and apple mixture to the pan. Increase the heat and cook for a minute then pour in cider or apple juice. Bring to the boil and cook for about 2 minutes, or until evaporated. Add the stock and cook until the chicken and sweet potato are cooked through. Check the seasoning and stir in the crème fraîche. Serve on its own, nothing else needed.

🥄 15 mins

🍲 30 mins

# MOROCCAN CHICKEN

1 tbsp olive oil

8 chicken thighs, skin on

1 large red onion, cut into wedges through the root

Zest and juice of 1 orange

2 tsp ras el hanout

200g (7oz) basmati rice

50g (2oz) sultanas

6 dried apricots, chopped

450ml (15floz) hot chicken stock

25g (1oz) shelled pistachios, roughly chopped

1 tbsp chopped parsley

1 tbsp chopped mint leaves

Salt and pepper

**Ras el hanout is a Moroccan spice mixture. The name means 'top of the shop' and authentic mixes can contain 100 spices. The ones more readily available can still contain 20 different spices, from fragrant rose petals and bitter cloves to cumin, coriander and cardamom.**

1. Preheat the oven to 190°C, fan oven 170°C, Gas mark 5.

2. Heat the oil in a large ovenproof frying pan with a lid. Add the chicken thighs and cook until browned all over. Remove from the pan and set aside.

3. Add the onion and cook for 5 minutes, or until beginning to soften. Stir in the orange zest and juice, ras el hanout, rice, sultanas, apricots and chicken stock. Season and place the chicken on top of the rice. Bring to the boil, cover and cook in the oven for 25–30 minutes, until the chicken is cooked through.

4. Serve scattered with the pistachios and herbs.

# BAKED MEATBALLS
*in* RICH TOMATO SAUCE

**SERVES 6**

🥄 30 mins

🍳 40 mins

## FOR THE MEATBALLS:

3 tbsp olive oil

3 onions, finely chopped

3 garlic cloves, crushed

2 chopped anchovy fillets (optional)

500g (1lb 2oz) beef mince

125g (4½oz) fresh breadcrumbs

1 tbsp dried oregano

1 egg

Salt and pepper

## FOR THE RICH TOMATO SAUCE:

3 thyme sprigs

1 x 400g (14oz) can chopped tomatoes

600ml (1 pint) passata

2 tbsp tomato purée

1 tbsp brown sugar

1 tbsp red wine vinegar

250g (9oz) mozzarella, drained and torn

**If you are not yet a convert to anchovies, rest assured they add a delicious, subtle, salty richness to a sauce. There are some really good ready-prepared meatballs on the market now, so if short of time just add to the home-made sauce.**

1. **For the meatballs:** heat 2 tablespoons of the oil in a large deep frying pan, add the onions and cook gently until softened but not coloured. Add the garlic and anchovy fillets, if using. Increase the heat and cook for a few minutes. Spoon half the onion mix into a large bowl and the other half into a small bowl.

2. When the reserved onions in the large bowl have cooled, add the beef mince, breadcrumbs, oregano and egg with plenty of seasoning. Mix with your hands, then using wet hands shape into 20 meatballs. Heat the remaining oil in the frying pan and brown the meatballs in batches, adding more oil, as you need – the meatballs should be almost cooked through. Spoon the meatballs out of the pan on to a plate.

3. Preheat the oven to 180°C, fan oven 160°C, Gas mark 4.

4. **For the rich tomato sauce:** wipe the frying pan clean and return the remaining cooked onions to the pan. Add the thyme, tomatoes, passata, tomato purée, brown sugar and red wine vinegar, and bring to a simmer. Bubble for 25 minutes until the sauce has reduced and thickened. Season to taste.

5. Return the meatballs to the pan.

6. Scatter the mozzarella on top. Bake in the oven for 30 minutes, or until the meatballs are piping hot and cooked through, and the cheesey top is golden and bubbling. Serve with a tomato and cucumber salad.

# ONION TART TATIN

50g (2oz) butter

2 tsp sunflower oil

1 onion, cut into wedges through the root

1 red onion, cut into wedges through the root

2 tbsp clear honey

2 tbsp balsamic vinegar

A few thyme sprigs

Salt and freshly ground black pepper

250g (9oz) ready-rolled puff pastry, defrosted if frozen

Rocket and goats' cheese, to serve

**This dish looks so impressive. Serve with a sprinkling of goats' cheese and rocket and your friends and family will be amazed and delighted.**

1. Melt the butter and oil in a 20cm (8in) ovenproof frying pan. Add the onions and cook over a medium heat for about 5 minutes, turning from time to time, until just beginning to brown.

2. Add the honey and balsamic vinegar and cook for a further 5 minutes, moving and shaking the pan occasionally so the onions do not stick to the pan. Arrange the onions so they make a pretty pattern remembering you will be inverting the tart. Add the thyme stems and season well. Leave to cool while you prepare the pastry.

3. Roll out the pastry on a lightly floured surface and cut into a circle slightly larger than the diameter of the frying pan.

4. Cover the onions with pastry and tuck down the sides of the pan. Make two small slits for the steam to escape.

5. Bake for 35–40 minutes until the pastry is well risen. Leave to stand for 5 minutes. Turn the pastry gently to release; you should be able to spin the tart tatin when it is ready to serve. Cover the pan with a plate, invert then remove the pan leaving the tart now on the plate. If there is any liquid still in the bottom of the pan, heat gently and pour over the onions. Serve warm or cold, with a scattering of rocket and goats' cheese.

# PUY LENTIL RAGU
## *with* MINTY YOGHURT

1 tbsp olive oil

1 onion, finely chopped

3 carrots, finely chopped

2 celery sticks, finely chopped

2 garlic cloves, crushed

150g (5oz) chestnut mushrooms, sliced

500g (1lb 2oz) Puy lentils, rinsed and drained

1 x 400g (14oz) can chopped tomatoes

2 tbsp tomato purée

2 tsp each dried oregano and thyme

1.5 litres (2½ pints) vegetable stock

150g (5oz) Greek yoghurt

2 tbsp chopped fresh mint

2 tbsp chopped fresh parsley

Squeeze of lemon juice

Salt and pepper

**Do you have a meatless day in your house? Add this to the list and I doubt any of your family will complain – comfort food at its best.**

1. Heat the oil in a large deep frying pan and add the onion, carrots, celery and garlic.

2. Cook gently for 15 minutes until everything is softened. Add the mushrooms and cook for a further 5 minutes. Stir in the lentils, chopped tomatoes, tomato purée, herbs and stock. Bring to the boil, turn the heat down to a gentle simmer and cook for 20–25 minutes until the lentils are tender and the sauce reduced slightly. Season to taste.

3. While the lentils are cooking, mix together the yoghurt and fresh herbs. Chill while the lentils are cooking.

4. Serve the lentils alongside the herby yoghurt and a squeeze of lemon juice.

# ONE PAN SPICED HADDOCK RICE

SERVES 4

🥄 15 mins

🍲 30 mins

1 tbsp sunflower oil

2 tbsp mild curry paste (such as korma)

1 small onion, finely chopped

300g (11oz) basmati rice, rinsed and drained

700ml (1¼ pints) hot vegetable or chicken stock, either fresh or made from a cube

250g–300g (9–11oz) skinless smoked haddock fillet, cut into bite-sized cubes

75g (3oz) frozen peas

Handful of parsley leaves, chopped

Lemon wedges, to serve

**Once you have mastered cooking rice dishes in a lidded frying pan your weekly repertoire will soon expand. This combines the wonderful warming flavours of curry and smoked fish. Add boiled eggs and you have kedgeree, a perfect Sunday brunch dish.**

1. Heat a large, deep lidded frying pan. Add the oil and curry paste and cook for a minute just to release the aromas. Add the onion and cook for 4–5 minutes or until it begins to soften. Add the rice to the pan and stir to coat in the curry paste. Pour in the stock, scraping the bottom of the pan to release all the goodness. Bring to the boil.

2. Cover the pan and turn the heat down to low. Leave the rice to simmer slowly for 12 minutes until all the liquid has been absorbed and the rice is cooked. Remove the lid and add the haddock and peas. Cover the pan and leave to stand for 7 minutes. The residual heat will cook the haddock and peas.

3. Serve scattered with the parsley and lemon wedges.

# LEEK, WALNUTS *and* BLUE CHEESE RISOTTO

4 walnut halves

25g (1oz) unsalted butter

1 tbsp olive oil

2 leeks, sliced

150g (5oz) risotto rice (Arborio or Carnaroli)

50ml (2floz) dry white wine

750ml (1¼ pints) vegetable stock, either fresh or made with 1½ stock cubes

75g (3oz) Dolcelatte cheese, cubed

50g (2oz) Parmesan cheese, grated

Salt and pepper

**Rather than toasting four walnut halves just for this recipe, toast a bagful and store ready to add to salads, porridge or crumbles.**

1. Heat a large frying pan over a medium-high heat. When the pan is hot, add the walnuts. Stir until the nuts just turn golden brown. Tip from pan, as they will continue to cook after being removed from the heat. When cool enough to handle, roughly chop.

2. Give the pan a quick wipe and add the butter and oil. Add the leeks and cook over a gentle heat for about 10–12 minutes, stirring every now and again, until the leeks are soft and translucent but not coloured.

3. Stir in the risotto rice until well coated in the pan juices and cook for 1–2 minutes, or until the rice grains start to turn translucent. Add the wine and cook for 3–4 minutes, or until nearly all of the liquid has evaporated.

4. Add a ladleful of the stock to the pan and stir well. Cook for 1–2 minutes, or until nearly all of the stock has been absorbed, then add another ladleful of the stock. Repeat the process until the rice has become plump and creamy but still has a little bite left in it, about 20 minutes.

5. Stir in the Dolcelatte and half the Parmesan and season to taste. Serve sprinkled with the remaining Parmesan and chopped walnuts.

# FISH CAKES *with* QUICK TARTARE SAUCE

**SERVES 4**

🥄 20 mins, plus chilling time

🍲 20 mins

## FOR THE FISH CAKES:

250g (9oz) skinless cod or haddock fillet, from a sustainable source

200g (7oz) skinless smoked cod or haddock, from a sustainable source

2 bay leaves

250ml (9floz) milk

350g (12oz) mashed potatoes

1 tsp capers, drained, dried and chopped

Zest of 1 lemon

1 tbsp chopped flat leaf parsley

1 tbsp chopped chives

Salt and Pepper

1 egg, lightly beaten

2 tbsp plain flour

85g (3½oz) panko crumbs

3–4 tbsp sunflower oil

## FOR THE QUICK TARTARE:

200ml (7floz) good-quality mayonnaise

3 tbsp capers, drained and chopped

3 tbsp gherkins, drained and chopped

1 small shallot, finely chopped

Squeeze of lemon juice

3 tbsp chopped parsley

**Ssshhh… don't tell anyone but I always keep a pack of instant mash potatoes in the cupboard – it's perfect for fish cakes.**

1. **For the fish cakes:** lay the fish and bay leaves and milk in a deep frying pan. Cover and bring to a gentle boil, lower the heat and simmer for 4 minutes. Take the pan off the heat and let stand, covered, for 10 minutes.

2. Lift the fish out of the milk with a slotted spoon and put on a plate to cool.

3. Mix together the mashed potatoes, capers, lemon zest, parsley and chives. Season well with salt and pepper.

4. Pat the fish dry with kitchen paper, break into chunks and add to the potatoes. Stir vey gently so you do not mash the fish too much. Leave to cool completely.

5. Pour the egg into one shallow bowl and put the flour in another shallow bowl. Spread the panko breadcrumbs on a baking sheet.

6. Divide the fish mixture into four and with floured hands, carefully shape into four cakes and roll in flour. One by one roll each cake in the egg, then the crumbs, making sure they are completely covered. Chill for at least 1 hour or longer if time allows.

7. **For the tartare sauce:** mix together all of the ingredients in a small bowl and season. Chill until ready to use.

8. Heat the oil in the frying pan. Cook the fish cakes over a medium heat for about 5 minutes on each side, or until crisp and golden. You may need to do this in batches.

9. Serve the fish cakes alongside the tartare sauce and with a crisp green salad.

# STICKY PAN FRIED SALMON

**SERVES 4**

🥄 10 mins

🍲 15 mins

1 tbsp soft brown sugar

1 tsp sumac

1 tbsp sesame seeds

1 tsp cornflour

4 skin-on salmon fillets

2 lemons, halved

1 tbsp sunflower oil

1 tbsp pomegranate molasses

4 tbsp pomegranate seeds

**Sumac is a tangy, lemony spice often used in Mediterranean and Middle Eastern cooking. Sprinkle over soups, houmous or salads or rub over meats or vegetables before grilling. This recipe uses it as a glorious rub for salmon.**

1. Preheat the oven to 200°C, fan oven 180°C, Gas mark 6.

2. Mix together the sugar, sumac, sesame seeds and cornflour and rub all over the salmon.

3. Heat an ovenproof frying pan over a high heat. Add the lemons cut side down and cook for 5 minutes, or until golden brown. Remove the lemons, leaving any juices in the pan. Add the oil to the pan and add the salmon; cook for 2 minutes. Turn over and cook for a further 2 minutes. Drizzle the pomegranate molasses over the salmon before transferring the frying pan to the oven.

4. Cook for a further 8–10 minutes depending on the thickness of the salmon. Serve the salmon sprinkled with the pomegranate seeds and alongside the charred lemons. Delicious served with Quinoa Crumble (page 129).

# PAD THAI

50g (2oz) salted peanuts

3 tbsp groundnut oil

2 garlic cloves, crushed

2 shallots, thinly sliced

1 red chilli, deseeded and finely chopped

200g (7oz) large raw prawns

3 eggs, beaten

2 x 200g (7oz) packets straight-to-wok noodles

3 tbsp tamarind paste

3 tbsp fish sauce

Juice of 1 lime

2 tbsp muscovado sugar

½ tsp sesame oil

6 spring onions, sliced

150g (5oz) beansprouts

150g (5oz) sugar snap peas, halved and blanched

Handful of coriander, to serve

1 spring onion, shredded, to serve

**Sour tamarind, fiery chilli and salty fish sauce make this a dish bursting with flavour. Ready-cooked noodles are a brilliant store-cupboard ingredient – add to soups or curries, or serve with stir-fries.**

1. Heat a large frying pan over a medium heat and add the peanuts. Toast for 1–2 minutes, or until golden brown. Remove from the pan and roughly chop. Wipe the pan clean with kitchen paper.

2. Heat the oil in the pan. Add the garlic, shallots and red chilli and cook for 30 seconds. Add the prawns and stir-fry for 6 minutes. Pour in the beaten eggs and stir-fry until they look scrambled. Lower the heat and add the noodles.

3. Mix together the tamarind paste, fish sauce, lime juice, sugar and sesame oil for the dressing.

4. Add the sliced spring onions, beansprouts and sugar snap peas to the pan and toss for 3–4 minutes. When ready to serve add the dressing and serve sprinkled with the peanuts, coriander and shredded spring onion.

# SEA BASS *with* BABY FENNEL *and* ORANGE SALAD

**SERVES 4**

🥄 10 mins

🍲 10 mins

1 fennel bulb, trimmed

4 oranges

4 red chicory

2 tbsp freshly chopped dill

5 tbsp olive oil

50g (2oz) pine nuts

4 sea bass fillets

Salt and pepper

**One of the simplest ways to prepare fish is to pan fry a skin-on fillet. It gives golden, crispy skin on the outside and flaky, moist meat on the inside – and it's cooked in a matter of minutes.**

1. Slice the fennel bulb thinly and tip into a bowl. Peel and segment three of the oranges and add to the fennel. Roughly tear the chicory into the bowl.

2. Zest and juice the remaining orange and mix with the chopped dill. Slowly add 4 tablespoons of the oil to make a dressing, whisking all the time. Season and taste the dressing and then pour over the salad and toss gently.

3. In a large frying pan, toast the pine nuts for 2–3 minutes until very lightly golden over a low medium heat, tossing often – keep an eye on them as they burn very easily. Remove from the pan and set aside.

4. Heat a tablespoon of olive oil in a large frying pan and add the fish, skin side down. Cook for 2 minutes, pressing the fish flat with a spatula to make sure you get an evenly crispy skin. Turn the fish over and baste the fish with the oil and cook for a further 2 minutes, depending on the thickness of the fish.

5. Serve the fish with the salad and sprinkled with the pine nuts.

# ONE PAN TOMATO *and* SPINACH PASTA

**SERVES 2**

🥄 5 mins

🍲 12 mins

200g (7oz) mixed cherry tomatoes, halved

200g (7oz) spaghetti, snapped in half

1 small onion, thinly sliced

3 garlic cloves, thinly sliced

1 red chilli, finely chopped

Zest and juice of 1 lemon

4 tbsp extra virgin olive oil

600ml (1 pint) boiling water

100g (4oz) spinach, washed and chopped

50g (2oz) Parmesan cheese, shaved

Sea salt and black pepper

**An incredible one pan dish, cooked in less than 15 minutes. This dish will solve many a midweek dinner dilemma.**

1. Put the tomatoes, spaghetti, onion, garlic, chilli and the lemon zest and juice in a large, deep frying pan. Pour over the olive oil and water.

2. Place the pan over a medium-high heat and bring to the boil. Stir the pasta using tongs to separate it and to make sure it does not stick to the bottom. Cook for 6 minutes, add the spinach, stir again and continue to cook for a further 3–5 minutes or until the pasta is cooked and the liquid has evaporated and created a sauce.

3. Remove the pan from heat and stir in half the Parmesan. Season with salt and pepper and serve sprinkled with the remaining Parmesan.

🔪 10 mins

🍲 10 mins

# ONE PAN TUNA PASTA PUTTANESCA

3 tbsp extra virgin olive oil, plus extra to serve

1 shallot, thinly sliced

2 garlic cloves, crushed

¼ tsp red chilli flakes (optional)

50g (2oz) kalamata olives, pitted and lightly crushed

2 anchovies, drained

1 x 400g (14oz) can chopped tomatoes

400ml (14floz) water

125g (4½oz) pasta e.g. fusilli

½ tsp salt

1 x 200g (7oz) tuna steak in spring water, drained and flaked

1 tbsp capers

Black pepper (optional)

4 tbsp chopped fresh parsley

**When the fridge is bare remember pasta puttanesca as it uses many storecupboard staples. It's important to melt the garlic, anchovies and olives so they release their natural oil as this flavours and seasons the tomato-based sauce.**

1. Heat the oil in a very large, deep frying pan over a medium heat. Add the shallot, garlic, chilli flakes, if using, olives and anchovies and cook for 7 minutes until the shallots are soft and the anchovies are melted.

2. Add the tomatoes, water, pasta and salt. Bring to the boil, stirring using tongs, making sure the pasta is separated and does not stick to the bottom of the pan. Boil for 8 minutes, or until the pasta is cooked and the liquid has nearly evaporated to create a sauce.

3. Do not overcook, and do not worry if there is extra liquid still in the pan. Turn the heat off, add the tuna and capers and stir to combine. Check the seasoning, adding black pepper if needed. Serve topped with lots of freshly chopped parsley and an extra drizzle of olive oil.

# CHEAT'S FRYING PAN LASAGNE

SERVES 4–6

🍴 15 mins

🍲 1¼ mins

1 tbsp olive oil

1 onion, chopped

1 carrot, diced

1 celery stick, diced

3 garlic cloves, diced

1 red pepper, deseeded and diced

½ tsp chilli flakes

450g (1lb) beef mince

1 beef stock cube

1 x 400g (14oz) can chopped tomatoes

2 tbsp tomato purée

1 x 125ml (4floz) red wine

4 lasagne sheets, snapped in half

300ml (10floz) crème fraîche

50g (2oz) grated Parmesan

A grating of nutmeg

1 ball mozzarella, drained

Salt and pepper

**This recipe came from having the craving for lasagne one evening. It gives you the lasagne feelgood factor when you don't have the time a 'proper' lasagne deserves.**

1. Heat the olive oil in a deep 28cm (11in) frying pan over a medium-high heat. Cook the onion, carrot and celery for about 4–5 minutes until soft but not coloured. Stir in the garlic, red pepper, salt and pepper and the chilli flakes. Cook for a further couple of minutes.

2. Add the beef mince, breaking the meat clumps. Cook until the mince is browned all over. Crumble in the beef stock cube and add the chopped tomatoes, tomato purée and red wine. Cover and bring to the boil, reduce the heat and simmer 30–40 minutes, stirring occasionally.

3. Ease the lasagne pieces into the sauce to create layers of lasagne. Don't worry too much about how this looks, or if the layers overlap. Cover and bring the dish to a simmer, and cook, shaking the pan occasionally, for about 20 minutes, or until the pasta is done.

4. Preheat the oven to 200°C, fan oven 180°C, Gas mark 6.

5. Mix together the crème fraîche, half the Parmesan and nutmeg, then spoon on top of the lasagne mix. Rip up the mozzarella ball and dot over the top. Finish by sprinkling over the remaining Parmesan.

6. Carefully move the pan to the oven and cook for a further 20 minutes, or until the cheese is melted and golden brown. Serve straight to the table with a crisp green salad and lots of fresh bread.

**SERVES 4**

🥄 15 mins

🍲 30 mins

# BAKED BACON
## *and* PEA RISOTTO

2 tbsp olive oil

200g (7oz) pack smoked bacon lardons

1 onion, chopped

25g (1oz) butter

300g (11oz) risotto rice (Arborio or Carnaroli)

60ml (2½floz) white wine (optional)

700ml (1¼ pints) hot chicken stock

150g (5oz) frozen peas

50g (2oz) Parmesan, grated

Lemon wedges, to serve

**Peas and bacon is such a classic flavour combination. If you don't have any bacon just top the risotto with a handful of shredded ham.**

1. Preheat the oven to 200°C, fan oven 180°C, Gas mark 6.

2. Heat the oil in a large, deep ovenproof frying pan. Add the bacon lardons and cook for 7 minutes until golden and crisp. Stir in the onion and butter and cook for 3–4 minutes until soft. Add the rice and stir until the rice is coated and glistening. Pour over the wine, if using, and cook for 2 minutes until absorbed.

3. Add the hot stock, and give the rice a quick stir. Cover with a tight-fitting lid and bake in the oven for 18 minutes until just cooked. Stir through the peas and return to the oven, uncovered, for 5 minutes. Stir in half the Parmesan. Serve sprinkled with the remainder of the Parmesan and the lemon wedges.

# CHICKEN TARRAGON PIE

SERVES 4–6

🥄 25 mins

🍲 40 mins, plus chilling time

25g (1oz) unsalted butter

1 tbsp olive oil

1 leek, thinly sliced

2 garlic cloves, crushed

6 boneless, skinless chicken thighs, cut into 5cm (2in) cubes

150g (5oz) chestnut mushrooms, wiped and sliced or halved

50ml (2floz) white wine

150ml (5floz) chicken stock

2 tsp dried tarragon

200ml (7floz) double cream

500g (1lb 2oz) ready-made puff pastry

2 egg yolks, lightly beaten

Crushed black pepper

**The combination of chicken and tarragon is delicious. Use ready-made puff pastry as only hardcore bakers make their own puff pastry.**

1. Heat a large ovenproof frying pan until hot and add the butter and oil. Add the leek and garlic and cook for 1 minute. Add the chicken pieces and cook for about 5 minutes, or until just coloured. Add the mushrooms and cook over a high heat for 2–3 minutes until just softened. Add the wine and boil until all the wine has evaporated.

2. Pour in the stock and bring to a simmer. Add the tarragon and cream and simmer for 5 minutes. Check the seasoning and then set pan aside to cool completely.

3. Preheat the oven to 200°C, fan oven 180°C, Gas mark 6.

4. Roll the pastry out on a lightly floured surface until it is 5cm (2in) wider than the frying pan and about 5mm (¼in) thick. Brush the edges of the cooled frying pan with the egg yolks. Cut a couple of 1cm (½in)-wide strips of pastry and stick them to the rim of the frying pan. Brush this with more egg yolk, then lay the pastry over the filling and crimp at the edges. Trim away any excess pastry. Brush the top of the pie with the remaining egg and sprinkle with black pepper. Make two slits in the top and use any excess pastry to decorate the pie.

5. Bake in the oven for 25 minutes, or until the pastry is crisp and golden and the filling is bubbling hot.

# ONE POT MINCED BEEF HOT POT

**SERVES 4**

🥄 20 mins

🍲 1½ hours

3 tbsp sunflower oil

2 onions, chopped

400g (14oz) minced beef

275g (10oz) swede, diced

2 carrots, chopped

2 parsnips, chopped

2 tbsp plain flour

500ml (15½floz) beef stock, made with a stock cube

1 tsp Worcestershire Sauce

2 tbsp tomato ketchup

1 tbsp cream of horseradish sauce

125g (4½oz) frozen peas

500g (1lb 2oz) potatoes, peeled and thinly sliced

15g (½oz) butter, melted

Salt and pepper

**Shepherd's Pie meets Hot Pot! This all-in-one dish keeps the washing up to a minimum, especially as you take the pan straight to the table to serve.**

1. Preheat the oven to 180°C, fan oven 160°C, Gas mark 4.

2. Heat 1 tablespoon of the oil in a large, deep ovenproof frying pan, add the onions and cook for about 8 minutes, or until soft and beginning to colour. Turn the heat to high and add the mince. Cook until browned, breaking up the clumps.

3. Add another tablespoon of oil and add the swede, carrots and parsnips. Cook for a couple of minutes stirring to cover with the oil. Add the flour and cook for a further minute. Pour in half the beef stock and stir to combine. Add the remaining stock, Worcestershire sauce, ketchup, horseradish sauce, seasoning and peas; bring to the boil and simmer for 5 minutes.

4. Take off the heat and stir. Lay the potato slices, overlapping slightly, on top and then brush with melted butter or oil. Cover and bake in the oven for 1 hour.

5. Remove the lid and continue to cook for a further 15 minutes, or until golden brown.

6. Serve on its own or with some crusty bread.

# SAUSAGE FENNEL STEW
## *with* DUMPLINGS

FOR THE SAUSAGE STEW:

3 tbsp olive oil

1 onion, finely diced

1 fennel bulb, finely chopped

4 garlic cloves, crushed

6 pork and apple sausages

4 sprigs rosemary chopped

1 tsp fennel seeds

150ml (5floz) red wine

1 x 400g (14oz) can chopped
tomatoes

1 tsp sugar

250ml (9floz) chicken stock

Salt and pepper

FOR THE DUMPLINGS:

100g (4oz) plain flour,
plus extra for dusting

½ tsp baking powder

Pinch of salt

50g (2oz) suet

**This dish is the epitome of comfort food. The pork and apple sausages give the dish an added sweetness, which marries beautifully with the fennel and the light fluffy dumplings.**

1. **For the sausage stew**: heat the oil in a large, deep-lidded frying pan. Add the onion, fennel and garlic. Cook for 5 minutes until beginning to soften. Split open the sausages and remove and discard the skin. Add the sausagemeat to the onion mix and gently cook, breaking up with a wooden spoon, until golden and beginning to crisp. Add the rosemary and fennel seeds and season generously. Add the wine, tomatoes, sugar and stock. Cover and cook on the lowest heat for 20 minutes.

2. **For the dumplings**: sift the flour, baking powder and salt into a bowl. Add the suet and enough water to form a dough. Once you have a soft dough stop mixing, as you don't want to overwork the dough. If it is too sticky, add a tiny bit more flour. With floured hands, roll spoonfuls of the dough into small balls.

3. Remove the lid from the stew and place the balls on top.

4. Cover, return to the oven and cook for a further 20 minutes, or until the dumplings have swollen and are tender. Check the seasoning before serving sprinkled with parsley.

# SAUSAGE *and* PEARL BARLEY STEW

**SERVES 4**

🥄 15 mins

🍲 50 mins

3 tbsp oil

6 Cumberland sausages

2 onions, sliced

2 celery sticks, halved lengthways and cut into chunks

2 carrots, diced

200g (7oz) pearl barley, rinsed with cold water

2 sprigs thyme, leaves removed

Approx. 900ml (1½ pints) chicken stock

½ savoy cabbage, roughly chopped

Zest of 1 lemon

Salt and pepper

**Pearl barley may have an old-fashioned image but it is a great ingredient to bulk out a dish and keep costs down. If you are making this stew in advance add a little more stock or water when you reheat it, as the pearl barley will have soaked up some of the sauce.**

1. Heat 2 tablespoons of the oil in a large deep frying pan. Add the sausages and cook for 8–10 minutes, turning every so often, until golden. Remove from the pan and set aside.

2. Add the remaining oil to the pan. Add the onion, celery and carrot and cook gently for 5–6 minutes, stirring now and then, until softened.

3. Stir in the pearl barley and thyme followed by the stock. Season well. Simmer for 10 minutes, and then return the sausages to the pan. Simmer for another 20 minutes.

4. Add the chopped cabbage and lemon zest and more water, if the liquid level is low. Simmer for another 5–10 minutes until the cabbage is just cooked. Check the seasoning and serve.

# PAN FRIED CHICKEN CAESAR SALAD *with* CHARRED LETTUCE

FOR THE CROÛTONS:

2 tsp olive oil

1 small garlic clove, crushed

1 tsp fresh thyme leaves, roughly chopped

¼ ciabatta loaf

Salt and pepper

FOR THE DRESSING:

1 garlic clove, crushed

2 anchovies, drained

75g (3oz) Parmesan, grated, plus extra to serve

5 tbsp mayonnaise

1 tbsp white wine vinegar

FOR THE SALAD:

2 skinless chicken breast fillets

2 tsp plain flour

1 tbsp vegetable oil

2 little gem lettuces, washed and quartered

**If you've never tried cooking lettuce like this before, it will be a revelation; the outside becomes charred and soft and the inside stays firm. If you want a carb-free salad leave out the croûtons.**

1. **For the croûtons:** mix together the olive oil with the crushed garlic and thyme and season. Tear the ciabatta into large croûtons and mix in the garlicky oil. Heat a large non-stick pan over a medium heat. Add half the ciabatta croûtons, cook for about 2 minutes, tossing occasionally until crisp and golden. Remove and tip on to a plate and repeat with the remaining croûtons.

2. **For the dressing:** put the garlic and anchovies into a small bowl and mash with a fork against the side. Add the Parmesan and mix with the mayonnaise and vinegar. Season to taste. If the dressing seems thick just add a little water to loosen the mix.

3. **For the salad:** place the chicken breasts one at a time between two sheets of greaseproof paper, then using the base of a pan flatten to 5mm (¼in) thick. Season with salt and freshly ground black pepper. Dust in flour to coat thoroughly, tapping away any excess.

4. Preheat the frying pan until smoking hot. Add a little oil and the chicken. Cook for 5 minutes, turn over and cook for a further couple of minutes, or until the chicken is cooked through. Wipe away any excess flour from the pan. Leave to rest.

5. Return the pan to a high heat. Drizzle the little gem wedges with oil. Place them cut sides down in the pan and cook for 2–3 minutes. They should just start to char not burn. Remove to a plate.

6. **To serve:** top the little chargrilled gem wedges and chicken with a drizzle of the dressing and add a handful croûtons. Sprinkle with extra Parmesan.

# SUMMER CHICKEN CASSEROLE

**SERVES 4**

🥄 15 mins

🍲 40 mins

1 tbsp olive oil

1 onion, sliced

1 fennel bulb, sliced

500g (1lb 2oz) boneless, skinless chicken thighs

300g (11oz) small new potatoes

500ml (15½floz) chicken stock

200g (7oz) tenderstem broccoli, trimmed

75g (3oz) green beans, fresh or frozen, trimmed

150g (5oz) peas, fresh or frozen

4 spring onions, sliced

4 little gems, halved

2 tbsp crème fraîche

Salt and pepper

**A stew is not just for winter. Make use of the best seasonal vegetables in this summer dish – broccoli, courgettes and broad beans all work beautifully.**

1. Heat the oil in a large lidded frying pan over a medium heat. Add the onion and fennel and cook gently for 5 minutes until soft but not coloured.

2. Add the chicken and cook until lightly coloured. Add the potatoes, stock and season well. Bring to the boil, reduce the heat, cover and simmer for 30 minutes until the potatoes are tender and the chicken is cooked.

3. Add the broccoli and green beans, cover and cook for 5 minutes. Add the peas, spring onions and little gems. Season and cook uncovered for a further 5 minutes. Add the crème fraîche and heat through. Serve immediately.

# SPICED TURKEY MINCE
## *with* QUINOA CRUMBLE

FOR THE SPICED TURKEY MINCE:

2 tbsp olive oil

500g (1lb 2oz) turkey mince

1 red onion, chopped

1 red pepper, deseeded
and finely chopped

2 tbsp plain flour

2 tsp ground cumin

2 tsp ground coriander

½ tsp ground cinnamon

1–2 green chillies, chopped

5cm (2in) piece fresh ginger,
grated

2 garlic cloves, crushed

400ml (14floz) fresh chicken
stock

227g (8oz) can chopped
tomatoes

FOR THE HERBY QUINOA
CRUMBLE:

250g (9oz) pouch mixed grains
with red rice and quinoa

2 tbsp extra virgin olive oil

150g (5oz) feta, crumbled

Zest of 1 lemon

Handful of fresh mint, leaves
sliced

Handful of fresh parsley,
leaves chopped

100g (4oz) pomegranate
seeds, to serve

**A savoury crumble made with the wonderful Middle Eastern
flavours and a crunchy quinoa topping. This is an oven-to-table
dish so forks to the ready.**

1. Preheat the oven to 190°C, fan oven 170°C. Gas mark 5.

2. **For the spiced turkey mince**: heat half the oil in a large non-stick
   frying pan. Add the turkey mince and cook until browned breaking
   up the clumps of mince with a spoon. Tip on to a plate and set aside.

3. Wipe out the pan with kitchen paper. Add the remaining olive
   oil and cook the onion and pepper gently over a low heat for
   8 minutes, or until soft but not coloured. Stir in the flour, spices,
   chillies, ginger and garlic and cook for 2 minutes. Return the
   mince to the pan, discarding any juices and pour in the stock and
   tomatoes. Bring to the boil, then turn down the heat and simmer
   for 25–30 minutes until the sauce has thickened.

4. **For the herby quinoa crumble**: tip the contents of the quinoa
   pouch into a large bowl add the oil, feta, lemon zest and half the
   herbs. Spoon over the turkey mixture and bake in the oven for
   20–25 minutes.

5. Serve sprinkled with the pomegranate seeds and remaining herbs.

# LEMON GARLIC *and* THYME PORK ESCALOPES

**SERVES 4**

🥄 15 mins

🍳 10 mins

100g (4oz) panko or dried breadcrumbs

Zest of 1 lemon

2 garlic cloves, finely chopped

1 tbsp fresh thyme leaves

2 tbsp flour

2 eggs, beaten

3 tbsp milk

4 pork loin steaks

50g (2oz) unsalted butter

1 tbsp light olive oil

Salt and freshly ground black pepper

**Zesty and crispy pork is quick to cook. This can also be made with flattened chicken or even rose veal.**

1. Mix together the breadcrumbs, lemon zest, garlic and thyme. Season and spread out on a large plate.

2. Sprinkle the flour on a separate plate and season.

3. Mix the eggs and milk in a shallow bowl.

4. Trim the fat from the steaks and one at a time place between two sheets of greaseproof paper, then use the base of a pan to flatten to 5mm (¼in) thick. Dip in the flour, then dip it in the egg wash, and then coat it in the breadcrumbs. Dip and coat the pork a second time, so that it's well coated with seasoned crumbs.

5. Repeat with the remaining pork steaks.

6. Heat a large frying pan over a medium heat and melt half the butter and add a drizzle of olive oil. When the butter is foaming, add the escalopes (you may need to do this is batches) and cook for about 4–5 minutes, or until golden brown, then turn them over and cook on the other side. They are cooked if the juices run clear when the pork is pierced with a skewer. Serve immediately with coleslaw and a crisp green salad.

DINNERS

# STEAK *with* PEPPERCORN SAUCE *and* PAN FRIED POTATOES

SERVES 2

🥄 20 mins

🍲 25 mins

FOR THE PAN FRIED POTATOES:

500g (1lb 2oz) waxy potatoes such as Maris Piper, Desirée or Charlotte

1 tbsp olive oil

Salt and pepper

FOR THE STEAKS:

2 sirloin, rib-eye or rump steaks

1 tbsp olive oil

Salt and pepper

FOR THE PEPPERCORN SAUCE:

6 tbsp good, hot beef stock

2 tbsp brandy

1 tbsp Worcestershire sauce

1 tbsp Dijon mustard

1 tsp whole black peppercorns, crushed

100ml (3½floz) double cream

Salt

1 tbsp chopped flatleaf parsley

**These pan-fried potatoes are a wonderful alternative to chips and so much simpler to prepare.**

1. **For the pan-fried potatoes**: cut the potatoes into chunks. Heat the oil in a pan over a medium-high heat and then add the potatoes in a single layer, cooking them in batches if necessary. Season and leave to cook undisturbed until golden brown. Turn over and repeat. Remove the potatoes from the oil and shake slightly; put on to a kitchen paper-lined tray and leave to cool. Season well. Repeat until all the potatoes have been cooked.

2. **For the steaks**: heat the frying pan, season the steaks and brush with the oil. Cook for 3–3½ minutes each side for a medium rare steak. Transfer to a warm serving plate, loosely cover with foil and keep warm.

3. **For the peppercorn sauce**: heat the frying pan again and add the stock; the stock should deglaze the pan making sure you get all the tasty goodness off the bottom. Bring to the boil and cook until reduced by half. Add the brandy, Worcestershire sauce, mustard, peppercorns and cream. Stir and bring to the boil over a high heat. Season with salt and cook until it reaches the consistency of pouring cream. Stir in the parsley.

4. Stir any meat juices from the steak plate into the sauce. Serve with the steaks and pan fried potatoes.

🔪 5 mins

🍲 35–40 mins

# TOAD IN THE HOLE

115g (4¼oz) plain flour

2 medium eggs

225ml (8floz) milk

1 tbsp wholegrain mustard

2 tbsp olive oil

4 large Cumberland sausages

1 red onion, sliced

Salt and pepper

**A childhood favourite that is very easy to make. Cooking the batter in the same pan that the sausages were fried in means that the batter is flavoured with the delicious sausage juices.**

1. Preheat the oven to 220°C, fan oven 200°C, Gas mark 7.

2. Put the flour, eggs and half the milk into a large bowl. Whisk slowly, gradually incorporating the flour from the edge of the bowl. Finally add the rest of the milk and mustard and whisk well. Season with salt and pepper.

3. Put the oil into a 25cm (10in) non-stick ovenproof frying pan. Add the sausages and onion and cook over a medium heat for 6–8 minutes, or until the sausages are evenly brown all over and the onion caramelised. Making sure the pan is very hot, pour the batter over the hot sausages and quickly put into the hot oven.

4. Reduce the temperature to 200°C, fan oven 180C, Gas mark 6 and cook for 25–35 minutes or until the batter is well risen and golden and the sausages are cooked. Serve immediately.

# THREE CHEESE *and* SPINACH FILO PIE

**SERVES 6**

🥄 20 mins

🍳 35 mins

250g (9oz) baby spinach

250g (9oz) ricotta cheese

2 tbsp chopped fresh mint

2 tbsp chopped fresh parsley

Grated zest of 1 lemon and juice of ½

2 medium eggs, beaten

200g (7oz) feta, crumbled

7 filo pastry sheets (270g/10oz pack)

50g (2oz) butter, melted, plus extra for greasing

50g (2oz) pine nuts, toasted

200g (7oz) roasted peppers, drained and sliced

50g (2oz) Cheddar cheese, grated

Salt and pepper

**A version of the Greek spanakopita. The ricotta and spinach are encased in layers of crisp filo pastry with an added sharpness from the roasted red peppers and crunch from the pine nuts.**

1. Preheat the oven to 200°C, fan oven 180°C, Gas mark 6. You need a 20cm (8in) deep non-stick ovenproof frying pan.

2. Place the spinach in a colander set in a large bowl. Pour over boiling water and shake dry. Pour over cold water and shake dry and squeeze to remove as much water as possible. Pat dry with kitchen paper, making sure the spinach is as dry as possible. Roughly chop.

3. Mix the ricotta, mint, parsley, lemon zest and juice, eggs and feta and season with salt and pepper.

4. Lay a sheet of baking parchment slightly bigger that the filo sheets on a surface and brush with melted butter, then lay one sheet of filo on the paper and brush with melted butter. Lay another layer of filo at a 90° angle across the first sheet and brush with melted butter. Lay the next sheet at a 45° angle and brush with melted butter. Continue until all the filo sheets have been used (or save some for later if you want to use fewer sheets for the pie). Using the paper to lift the pastry, ease into the pan with the excess filo overhanging the sides of the pan.

5. Spoon half the ricotta mix into the pan, followed by the dry spinach, a sprinkling of the pine nuts and then the chopped peppers. Top with the remaining ricotta mix and finish with a layer of Cheddar cheese. Fold the pastry over the top, scrunching to seal. Use any leftover filo to bridge the gap in the top. This does not have to look neat so do not worry too much. Brush the pastry all over with more melted butter.

6. Bake for 35 minutes until golden and set. Leave to cool before using the baking parchment to ease the pie out of the pan. Serve in slices with a crisp green salad.

# DESSERTS *and* BAKING

# CORNBREAD

200g (7oz) cornmeal
or yellow polenta

250ml (9floz) buttermilk

50g (2oz) butter

1 tbsp soft light brown sugar

1 tsp baking powder

¼ tsp bicarbonate of soda

1 tsp salt

2 large eggs, lightly beaten

Pinch of chilli flakes (optional)

**This is a bread that crosses the sweet/savoury divide. Omit the chilli flakes and serve with butter and jam, but it's best served with spicy dishes such as chilli or barbecue spare ribs.**

1. Preheat the oven to 220°C, fan oven 200°C, Gas mark 7.

2. Toast the cornmeal in a dry frying pan until fragrant, then mix half with the buttermilk and leave to soak for at least 1 hour or longer if time allows.

3. Melt the butter in a 20cm (8in) non-stick ovenproof frying pan and cook until the butter just starts to turn brown.

4. Stir together the remaining toasted cornmeal with the sugar, baking powder, bicarbonate of soda, salt, eggs and chilli flakes, if using. Add the soaked cornmeal and whisk together. Add the hot butter and stir to combine.

5. Heat the frying pan and very carefully pour in the cornmeal batter.

6. Bake for 20–25 minutes, or until a skewer inserted into the centre of the bread comes out clean. Serve warm.

# FRYING PAN BREAD

500g (1lb 2oz) strong white flour, plus extra for dusting

2 tsp salt

7g (¼oz) sachet fast action yeast

3 tbsp olive oil

300ml (10floz) water

**Once you have mastered this basic white bread recipe you can adapt it to make wholemeal, granary or flavoured bread.**

1. Put the flour in a large bowl. Add the salt one side and the yeast on the other. Make a well in the centre, then add the oil and water, and mix well.

2. Tip the dough on to a lightly floured surface and knead for about 10 minutes, or until the dough is silky smooth. This can also be done in a stand mixer with a dough hook in half the time. Put the dough in a clean oiled bowl and cover with cling film.

3. Leave to prove in a warm place for 1 hour, or until doubled in size.

4. Lightly flour a deep 20cm (8in) non-stick ovenproof frying pan.

5. When the dough is ready and risen, scrape it from the bowl and turn it on to a lightly floured surface. Knead the dough roughly for a few minutes, gently fold and mould it into a ball and place in the frying pan. Leave to prove for a further hour, or until it's doubled in size and filling the frying pan.

6. Preheat the oven to 220°C, fan oven 200°C, Gas mark 7.

7. Dust the loaf with flour and make a couple of cuts in the top of the loaf. Bake for 25–30 minutes until golden brown and the loaf sounds hollow when tapped underneath. Cool on a wire rack.

# NO-KNEAD ROSEMARY
## *and* OLIVE FOCACCIA

SERVES 6–8

⌒ 20 mins, plus up to
24 hours proving

30 mins

400g (14oz) strong white bread flour

1 tsp fast action dried yeast

2 tbsp olive oil, plus extra for greasing

1 tbsp flaky sea salt

250ml (9floz) warm water

3 rosemary sprigs, roughly chopped

100g (4oz) pitted green olives in herb dressing, drained and sliced

**This recipe takes a while to prove, but the hands-on involvement during that time is minimal. For a crunchy crust and soft crumb, it's definitely worth the wait.**

1. Mix together the flour, yeast, 1 tablespoon of olive oil and 1 teaspoon of salt into a large bowl. Add the warm water and mix thoroughly with a wooden spoon to make a sticky dough. Cover with cling film and put in the fridge for at least 10 hours, or if possible leave for up to 24 hours. If the dough looks like it might rise out of the bowl just squash it down.

2. When the dough is bubbly and has doubled in size, remove from the fridge and leave at room temperature for 1 hour.

3. Oil a 24cm (9½in) heavy-based non-stick ovenproof frying pan. With oiled hands, fold the sides of the dough in one at a time in the bowl; tip the dough over into the pan seam side down.

4. Use your fingertips to create dimples in the dough, press in the chopped rosemary and olive slices and spread the dough to the sides of the pan. Scatter over the remaining salt and drizzle with the remaining olive oil. Cover with cling film and leave to rise for 1 hour, or until almost doubled in size.

5. Preheat the oven to 220°C, fan oven 200°C, Gas mark 7.

6. Uncover the dough and bake on the middle shelf for 30 minutes until well risen and golden brown. Using a thin spatula, loosen the focaccia and peek underneath. If the bottom is not as crisp as you would like, place the pan on the hob and cook for 1–3 minutes over a medium heat, moving the pan around to cook evenly.

7. Cool for 10 minutes in the pan before transferring to a wire rack. Best eaten warm.

# DROP SCONES *and*
# RHUBARB BERRY COMPÔTE

MAKES 8

20 mins

30 mins

FOR THE DROP SCONES:

200g (7oz) plain flour

1 tsp baking powder

Pinch of fine salt

4 tbsp caster sugar

2 large eggs, lightly beaten

25g (1oz) unsalted butter, melted, plus extra for frying

200ml (7floz) semi-skimmed milk

1 tbsp oil, for frying

FOR THE RHUBARB AND BLUEBERRY COMPÔTE:

450g (1lb) rhubarb, trimmed and cut into 2cm (1in) pieces

200g (7oz) strawberries, hulled and halved

150g (5oz) blueberries

100g (4oz) caster sugar

1 cinnamon stick

1 star anise

1 vanilla pod, split lengthways and seeds removed

Zest and juice of 1 orange

Crème fraîche, to serve

**If you have any compôte left over serve it with your breakfast porridge.**

1. Make the compôte first so the flavours have time to develop. Place the rhubarb, berries, sugar, spices and the orange zest and juice into a large deep frying pan. Cook over a medium heat for about 10 minutes, stirring occasionally, or until the berries have released their juices and the rhubarb is soft.

2. Strain the fruit through a fine sieve set over a bowl. Transfer the fruit and spices to a bowl. Return the juices to the pan, and bring to the boil over a high heat. Reduce to a simmer and cook until the liquid has thickened slightly. Pour the sauce over the fruit and stir to combine; let it cool to room temperature. Discard the whole spices. Wash the frying pan.

3. **For the drop scones**: sift the flour, baking powder and salt into a mixing bowl and stir in the sugar. Make a well in the middle; add the eggs, butter and a good splash of the milk. Whisk until thick and smooth, then whisk in the remaining milk.

4. Heat the frying pan, then add the butter and oil and swirl it around. Drop in 2–3 tablespoons of the batter, spacing them well apart, to allow for spreading. Cook for about 2 minutes, or until bubbles appear on the surface, flip the drop scones and cook until puffed in the middle. Keep warm while you cook another batch. Repeat with the remaining batter.

5. Serve the drop scones with a generous spoonful of the compôte and a dollop of crème fraîche.

**MAKES 12–14**

🔪 20 mins

🍲 5–10 mins

# WELSH CAKES (CACENNAU CRI)

225g (8oz) self-raising flour, sifted

110g (4¼oz) salted Welsh butter, plus extra for greasing

85g (3½oz) caster sugar, plus extra for dusting

50g (2oz) sultanas

½ tsp mixed spice

1 egg

Milk, if needed

**These little Welsh gems are easy to make and so very, very delicious. No point giving storage advice as they never last long enough.**

1. Place the flour into a large bowl, add the butter and rub in until it resembles fine breadcrumbs. Add the sugar, sultanas, mixed spice and then the egg. Mix to combine until you get a soft dough, adding a splash of milk if needed.

2. Roll the dough out on a lightly floured surface to a thickness of about 1cm (½in). Cut into rounds with a 6cm (2½in) cutter. Rub a heavy-based frying pan with butter and wipe the excess away; place over a medium heat. Cook the Welsh cakes in batches for 2–3 minutes each side or until golden brown and crisp and cooked through.

3. Remove the cakes from the pan and dust with caster sugar while still warm.

# BLACKBERRY CLAFOUTIS

SERVES 4

🥄 10 mins

🍲 40 mins

25g (1oz) butter

300g (11oz) blackberries

75g (3oz) caster sugar

2 medium eggs

50g (2oz) plain flour

100ml (3½floz) double cream

100ml (3½floz) semi-skimmed milk

Zest of 1 orange

1 tbsp icing sugar, for dusting

**Traditionally made with cherries, this soft, baked light batter surrounds the fruits, marrying the sweet batter with sharp seasonal blackberries.**

1. Preheat the oven to 180°C, fan oven 160°C, Gas mark 4.

2. Heat a 24cm (9½in) deep non-stick ovenproof frying pan and add the butter, berries and 1 tablespoon of caster sugar. Toss gently until the butter has just melted.

3. In a bowl, whisk the eggs and remaining sugar until thickened and creamy. Sift over the flour and then beat into the egg mixture. Whisk in the cream, milk and orange zest.

4. Pour the mixture over the berries and bake for 35–40 minutes until just set and golden. Serve warm with a dusting of icing sugar and lots of cream or custard.

🔪 20 mins

🍲 30 mins

# PEAR *and* GINGER TART TATIN

4 pears

375g (13oz) ready-rolled puff pastry

150g (5oz) caster sugar

25ml (1floz) water

25g (1oz) butter

Pinch of salt

1 piece stem ginger, finely chopped

4 cardamom pods, crushed and seeds removed

Crème fraîche, to serve

**Tart Tatin is a good dessert to perfect – once you have conquered the caramel it is relatively simple to make. For the apple version, use firm tart apples such as Cox's or Granny Smith.**

1. Peel, halve and core the pears, then put in the fridge, uncovered, until ready to use.

2. Unroll the pastry and roll a little thinner. Cut out a circle slightly larger than the pan. Chill in the fridge until ready to use.

3. Put the sugar and water into a 20cm (8in) non-stick ovenproof frying pan and leave to soak for a couple of minutes. Cook over a medium heat until golden and fudgy. Take off the heat and stir in the butter, salt, ginger and cardamom. Mix until well combined, and then carefully arrange the pears in the pan, cut-side down. Be careful, as the caramel will be hot. You may need to cut one of the pear halves into chunks to fill in the gaps. Return to the heat and cook for 5 minutes, then take off the heat and allow to cool completely.

4. Preheat the oven to 200°C, fan oven 180°C, Gas mark 6.

5. When the pears are cool, put the pastry on top of the pan and tuck in the edges around the pears. Make two slits in the pastry. Bake for about 30 minutes until the pastry is golden, and then remove from the oven. Allow to cool for 5 minutes. When cool enough to handle, ease the pastry round in a circle to release the pears and caramel. Place a plate, slightly larger than the pan, on top and then, very carefully, using oven gloves if needed, invert the tart on to the plate. Best served warm, with crème fraîche

# APPLE *and* MARZIPAN PIE

**SERVES 6–8**

🥄 20 mins

🍳 50 mins

5 (approx 550g/1lb 3oz) Granny Smith apples, peeled and sliced

4 (approx 800g/1lb 12oz) Braeburn apples, peeled and sliced

50g (2oz) caster sugar, plus extra for sprinkling

1 tsp ground cinnamon

500g (1lb 2oz) shortcrust pastry

1 egg, lightly beaten

100g (4oz) marzipan

**The wonderful mix of Braeburn and Granny Smith apples creates the perfect bite and the marzipan adds another layer of richness.**

1. Preheat the oven to 200°C, fan oven 180°C, Gas mark 6. You also need a 24cm (9½in) deep ovenproof heavy-based frying pan.

2. Toss the chopped apples in the sugar and cinnamon.

3. On a lightly floured surface, cut off a third of the pastry and set aside to make the lid. Roll the rest of the pastry big enough to generously line the frying pan. Use the rolling pin to help lift the pastry into the pie dish and gently press it into the sides, leaving any excess pastry overhanging the sides. Place in the fridge or better still the freezer, to chill for 10 minutes.

4. Roll out the remaining pastry to form the pastry lid. Use any excess to form shapes to decorate the pie. Chill until ready to use.

5. Remove the pastry base from the fridge or freezer and brush the bottom with a little of the beaten egg. Drain the apples and spread half the apple into the pastry case, then dot over the marzipan. Add the remaining apple mixture on top. Brush the edges with the egg.

6. Place the pastry lid on top, tucking the lid inside the base of the pastry, and crimp the edges to seal. Make two holes in the centre to allow steam to escape. Place any decorative shapes on top and then glaze with beaten egg. Sprinkle with a little extra sugar.

7. Bake in the oven for about 50 minutes. Check after 25 minutes and, if necessary, cover with foil to prevent the pastry edges from burning.

8. Serve the apple pie with old-fashioned custard.

# ORANGES *in* STAR ANISE CARAMEL

SERVES 4

7 mins

10 mins

4 oranges

75g (3oz) caster sugar

270ml (9½floz) water

2 star anise

50ml (2floz) Cointreau (optional)

Juice of ½ lemon

2 tbsp shredded mint leaves

**A simple dessert – but sometimes simple is best.**

1. Slice off the top and bottom of the oranges and sit them on a chopping board. With a sharp knife, slice off the peel and pith. Tip any juice into a bowl. Cut the oranges into slices, discarding any pips. Put the orange slices in a shallow bowl. Take a few strips of peel and with sharp knife slice away the pith and shred the peel finely.

2. Place the sugar and half the water in deep frying pan. Heat gently until the sugar is dissolved but not boiling. Once the sugar has dissolved, increase the heat and bring the mixture to the boil, continue to boil until the mixture turns a dark caramel colour. Add a little water, then wait for the spitting to calm down before adding the rest of the water. Add the star anise, orange peel and Cointreau, if using. Cook for 3 minutes.

3. Remove from the heat and pour over the oranges. Leave to marinate for at least an hour but can be for longer.

4. Remove the star anise before serving the oranges sprinkled with the mint leaves.

# POACHED PEARS *with* SALTED CARAMEL SAUCE

FOR THE SALTED CARAMEL SAUCE:

200g (7oz) caster sugar

125ml (4½floz) water

100g (4oz) unsalted butter

125ml (4½floz) double cream

1 tsp sea salt

FOR THE POACHED PEARS:

500ml (15½floz) water

200g (7oz) caster sugar

2 strips lemon zest

4 firm pears, peeled, cored and halved

**Add as much or as little salt to the caramel to suit your taste. Use immediately or pour into a jar and keep in the fridge for up to two weeks.**

1. **For the salted caramel**: put the sugar in a large deep non-stick frying pan. Pour over the water, trying to wet all the sugar. Swirl the pan and cook over a medium heat until the sugar disappears and begins to brown. After about 6 minutes the mixture should turn a dark amber colour; take off the heat and whisk in the butter until completely melted. Stir in the cream and most of the sea salt. Once cool enough, taste, adding more salt if you like.

2. **For the poached pears**: heat the water and sugar in the frying pan. Add the lemon zest. Slide in the pears cut side down and cover with a circle of baking paper, with a small hole cut in the centre.

3. Keep the liquid at a very low boil and simmer the pears for 15–25 minutes, or until tender all the way through when pierced with a cocktail stick.

4. Remove the pears with a slotted spoon. Increase the heat and boil rapidly to reduce the poaching liquid by half. Serve the pears in a pool of caramel and drizzled with the poaching liquid.

# TOASTED OATY PLUM CRUMBLE

SERVES 4–6

15 mins

30 mins

500g (1lb 2oz) fresh dark plums, stones removed and chopped

4 tbsp caster sugar

1 tbsp cornflour

Pinch of freshly grated nutmeg

1 vanilla pod, split and seeds scraped out

2 cinnamon sticks

FOR THE CRUMBLE TOPPING:

50g (2oz) jumbo oats

190g (7oz) plain flour

50g (2oz) Demerara sugar

100g (4oz) butter, softened

**This crumble is a celebration of plums and spice. Toasting the oats just adds to the party, giving the crumble an added crunchy and nutty texture.**

1. Preheat the oven to 200°C, fan oven 180°C, Gas mark 6.

2. Heat a dry 20cm (8in) deep ovenproof frying pan over a medium-high heat and add the oats for the crumble topping. Toast the oats until fragrant and with a hint of colour. Remove the oats to use later.

3. Add the plums to the pan and sprinkle with the sugar, cornflour and nutmeg. Add the vanilla seeds and cinnamon sticks.

4. Heat over a medium heat until the juices are starting to release. Give the plums a gentle stir.

5. **For the crumble topping**: mix the flour and sugar together in a bowl. Rub in the butter with your fingers until the mixture resembles coarse breadcrumbs. Stir in the toasted oats.

6. Sprinkle the crumble over the plums and bake in the oven for 35 minutes until golden brown.

7. Serve with crème fraîche or double cream.

# SPICED RHUBARB
*and* ALMOND COBBLER

## FOR THE SPICED RHUBARB:

700g (1½lb) rhubarb, trimmed and chopped into 3cm (1¼in) lengths

85g (3½oz) caster sugar

3cm (1¼in) piece fresh ginger, peeled and shredded

1 star anise

Zest and juice of 1 orange

## FOR THE TOPPING:

100g (4oz) plain flour, plus extra for dusting

50g (2oz) ground almonds

85g (3½oz) sugar

1 tsp baking powder

50g (2oz) butter, cold

Pinch of salt

75ml (2½floz) buttermilk

1 tsp vanilla extract

25g (1oz) Demerara sugar

25g (1oz) flaked almonds

**This is a super easy, lightly spiced rhubarb cobbler. Make the stewed rhubarb in advance and top with the cobbler and bake just before guests arrive. The house will be filled with a rich wonderful aroma.**

1. Preheat the oven to 180°C, fan oven 160°C, Gas mark 4.

2. **For the spiced rhubarb**: put the rhubarb and sugar into a 24cm (9½in) deep frying pan. Add the ginger, star anise, orange juice and zest. Cover, bring to the boil and simmer for a few minutes. Remove the lid and simmer for around 5 more minutes until the rhubarb has softened slightly. Remove the star anise or at least warn your guests it is there.

3. **For the topping**: place the flour, ground almonds, sugar, baking powder, butter and salt in a food processor. Pulse to a fine crumb. Add the buttermilk and pulse until the mixture starts to come together. Do not over process. Turn the dough out on to a lightly floured surface, and then gently knead to bring the mixture together. Roll into a sausage measuring 20cm (8in) by 4cm (1¾in) and cut into nine slices. Roll into flattened balls and place on top of the warm fruit and sprinkle with Demerara sugar and flaked almonds. Bake in the oven for 20–25 minutes or until the biscuits are golden brown. Cover the top loosely with a piece of foil if the biscuits are getting too dark.

4. Serve with ice cream, double cream or custard.

# RHUBARB *and* RASPBERRIES OPEN TART

**SERVES 4**

🥄 30 mins

🍲 55 mins

320g (11½oz) ready-rolled shortcrust pastry

75g (3oz) ground almonds

100g (4oz) caster sugar, plus 1 tbsp to sprinkle

400g (14oz) rhubarb, cut into 1cm (½in) chunks

125g (4½oz) raspberries

1 egg, lightly beaten

**This tart requires no fluting or crimping. It is the easiest tart ever. The ground almonds should help to avoid a soggy bottom.**

1. Preheat the oven to 200°C, fan oven 180°C, Gas mark 6.

2. On a lightly floured surface, roll the pastry slightly thinner than it is already. Cut into a circle 5cm (2in) larger than the frying pan. Ease the pastry into a 20cm (8in) non-stick ovenproof frying pan, allowing the pastry to hang over the edge. Spoon the ground almonds into the bottom of the pastry and top with half the sugar. Spoon in the rhubarb and raspberries and sprinkle with the remaining caster sugar.

3. Fold the excess pastry over the fruit (to create pleats). Lightly brush the top of the pastry with the egg and sprinkle with the remaining tablespoon of sugar. Bake for about 25–30 minutes or until golden brown. Leave to cool for 5–10 minutes. Slice into wedges and serve with ginger-flavoured cream or ice cream.

# PINEAPPLE UPSIDE DOWN CAKE

SERVES 6–8

🥄 20 mins

🍲 45 mins

150g (5oz) golden syrup

1 x 432g (15oz) tin pineapple slices in natural juices, drained, reserving 2 tbsp juice

50g (2oz) desiccated coconut

175g (6oz) butter, softened

175g (6oz) sugar

3 eggs, lightly beaten

175g (6oz) self-raising flour

**Some dishes are best left in the 70s but this one is still a classic. I've tinkered a little with my mum's recipe by adding coconut, but I still like the simplicity of the original. Make individual ones and your guests will definitely have a smile on their faces.**

1. Preheat the oven to 180°C, fan oven 160°C, Gas mark 4. The method is the same whether you are making individual or one large cake.

2. You need one 24cm (9½in) non-stick ovenproof deep frying pan or 6 x 12cm (4¾in) wide individual ovenproof frying pans.

3. Place the frying pan over a medium heat, and add the golden syrup. Heat until covering the base of the frying pan. Add the pineapple slices and arrange nicely. Sprinkle over half the desiccated coconut and set aside.

4. Put the butter, sugar, eggs and flour in a bowl and beat together until light and fluffy. Add the rest of the desiccated coconut and the reserved pineapple juice. The simplest way to make this cake is with an electric mixer, but you can use a wooden spoon as long as the butter is very soft.

5. Spoon the batter evenly over the pineapple and spread carefully so not to disturb the pineapple. Bake for 35–40 minutes or, if making individual cakes, bake for 20 minutes.

6. To check the cake is cooked press the cake lightly and if it springs back or if a skewer inserted in the centre comes out clean and dry, it is done.

7. Remove from the oven and cool the cake in the pan. Once the pan is cool enough to handle, ease the cake away from the edges using a plastic spatula and turn the cake out on to a plate. Serve either with a cup of tea or a jug of custard.

🥄 15 mins

🍲 35 mins

# CHOCOLATE BANANA CAKE

125g (4½oz) unsalted butter

175g (6oz) light brown sugar

2 eggs

3 ripe bananas, roughly mashed

1 tsp vanilla bean paste

80ml (2½floz) buttermilk

1 tbsp very strong coffee

125g (4½oz) self-raising flour

1 tsp baking powder

½ tsp salt

50g (2oz) dark chocolate chunks or chips

**No messy mixing bowl, just make and cook in the frying pan. What could be easier? Once word of advice, as this recipe calls for a non-stick pan make sure your whisk is not a metal one.**

1. Preheat the oven to 180°C, fan oven 160°C, Gas mark 4.

2. Melt the butter in a 24cm (9½in) non-stick ovenproof frying pan. Stir in the sugar and remove from the heat. Whisk until thoroughly combined. Allow the mixture to stand and cool for about 5 minutes. Make sure the mixture is cool enough before you add the eggs or they will scramble when added.

3. As the sugar and butter mixture cools it will look a bit clumpy, greasy and broken. Once the eggs are added the mix will come together. Add the eggs and whisk together until smooth. The mixture will be glossy and no longer greasy. Add the banana, vanilla bean paste, buttermilk and coffee.

4. Add the flour, baking powder and salt and carefully stir until all of the dry ingredients are incorporated. Fold in the chocolate chunks.

5. Bake for 40 minutes, or until a knife inserted into the centre comes out clean. Leave to cool and then serve.

# PLUM CAKE

SERVES 8

🥄 10 mins

🍳 45 mins

2–3 ripe plums

200g (7oz) unsalted butter, softened

250g (9oz) caster sugar

Zest of 1 orange

¼ tsp ground cinnamon

½ tsp ground ginger

2 large eggs

200ml (7oz) soured cream

300g (11oz) self-raising flour

1 level tsp baking powder

FOR THE ORANGE SYRUP:

50g (2oz) caster sugar

Juice of 1 orange made up to 100ml with water

1 tbsp Grand Marnier (optional)

**Make this when plums are in season and they are soft and juicy. Don't skimp on the ginger in the cake as it complements the plums beautifully.**

1. Butter a 24cm (9½in) deep non-stick ovenproof frying pan. Cut one long strip of baking paper about 2.5cm (1in) wide and lay in the bottom of the pan. Place to cover any rivets that you may have in the pan. Place a circle of baking paper over the strip.

2. Halve the plums and remove the stones. Place the plums cut side down on a chopping board and slice from top to bottom. Cover until ready to use.

3. Cream the butter, sugar, orange zest, cinnamon and ginger until light and fluffy. Add the eggs, one at a time, and beat well until combined. This is easiest done with an electric mixer but can be done by hand as long as the butter is very soft. Pour in the soured cream and beat well. If the mixture looks a little curdled add a spoonful of the flour. Sift in the flour and baking powder and gently mix in until thoroughly combined. Spoon into the pan and level with the back of a spoon.

4. Arrange the plum slices on top of the cake. Bake in the oven for 45–50 minutes, or until a skewer inserted in the centre comes out clean and dry. While the cake is baking make the orange syrup.

5. **For the orange syrup**: mix the sugar and orange juice in a small frying pan and stir over a low heat until the sugar dissolves. Bring to the boil, then reduce the heat and simmer for 10 minutes, or until the syrup thickens slightly. Add the Grand Marnier, if using.

6. When the cake is cooked, remove from the oven. While the cake is still warm pierce the surface with a cocktail stick and drizzle with the syrup.

# BREAD *and* BUTTER PUDDING

**SERVES 6–8**

⟾ 10 mins, plus 30 mins standing

🍲 35 mins

100g (4oz) sultanas

Zest and juice of 1 orange

4 eggs

75g (3oz) caster sugar

150ml (5floz) double cream

600ml (1 pint) whole milk

1 tbsp vanilla bean paste

1 slightly stale brioche loaf, cubed (approx. 300g/11oz bread)

50g (2oz) unsalted butter

¼ tsp grated nutmeg

¼ tsp ground cinnamon

2 tbsp Demerara sugar

**A rich, delicious pudding with a soft custard and crunchy crust on top. Stale bread or panettone work just as well as the brioche.**

1. Preheat the oven to 180°C, fan oven 160°C, Gas mark 4.

2. Soak the sultanas in the orange juice for 10 minutes.

3. To make the custard, place the eggs, sugar, double cream and milk in a very large bowl and whisk together until well mixed. Stir in the vanilla bean paste and drained soaked sultanas. Add the brioche cubes and gently press down into the liquid. Leave to stand for about 30 minutes.

4. After 30 minutes, put the butter into a 24cm (9½in) heavy-based ovenproof frying pan and place in the oven until the butter is melted and starting to bubble. Very carefully remove the pan from the oven and add the nutmeg, cinnamon and orange zest.

5. Spoon the soaked brioche and custard into the hot pan (being very careful as the pan will be hot) and sprinkle with Demerara sugar. Bake in the oven for 35 minutes, or until the custard has set and the top is golden brown. Serve with fresh cream or crème fraîche.

**SERVES 2–4**

🔪 5 mins

🍳 10 mins

# CHOCOLATE HAZELNUT QUESADILLAS

3 tbsp caster sugar

1 tbsp ground cinnamon

3–4 tbsp hazelnut chocolate spread

8 flour tortillas

2 tbsp butter

**Perfect for those 9pm munchies, or the 2pm munchies, or any time of the day munchies!!**

1. In a small bowl combine the sugar and cinnamon.

2. Spread the chocolate spread over one half of each tortilla. Fold each tortilla in half.

3. Preheat a non-stick frying pan and add half the butter. Add the tortillas to the pan two at a time and cook on both sides until golden brown.

4. Remove from the pan and sprinkle with the cinnamon sugar. Add more butter to the pan and cook the remaining tortillas. Serve immediately.

# PEANUT BUTTER BROWNIE

SERVES 6–8

🥄 10 mins

🍲 25 mins

115g (4¼oz) unsalted butter, cut into small cubes

125g (4½oz) dark 70% cocoa chocolate, finely chopped

1–2 tsp milk

170g (6oz) caster sugar

2 large eggs

1 tsp vanilla bean paste

90g (3¾oz) plain flour

½ tsp sea salt

2 tbsp peanut butter

**Made and cooked in the frying pan – no bowl needed! Brownies need to be gooey inside so be brave and take them out of the oven when the middle still looks soft as the brownies will continue cooking for a while once out of the oven.**

1. Preheat the oven to 180°C, fan oven 160°C, Gas mark 5.

2. Melt the butter in a 24cm (9½oz) non-stick deep ovenproof frying pan. Remove the pan from the heat and add the chocolate. Set the pan aside and leave the butter and chocolate mixture to sit for 5 minutes, and then stir to evenly combine. The chocolate should be melted and the mixture should be smooth.

3. Add the sugar and whisk to combine. Whisk in the eggs, one at a time. Add the vanilla bean paste and whisk vigorously for about 1 minute. Stir in the flour and salt, using a plastic spatula to clean the edges of the pan.

4. Mix the peanut butter in its jar to loosen and soften slightly. Spoon dollops of peanut butter all over the top. Using a knife, gently swirl into the batter.

5. Bake for 25–30 minutes, or until the edges look firm and well baked; the centre should be moist but not gooey. Do not overcook.

6. Leave to cool completely in the pan before cutting into squares.

🥄 40 mins

🍲 20 mins

# LEMON MERINGUE PIE

320g (11½oz) ready-rolled shortcrust pastry

1 x 394g (13½oz) can full-fat condensed milk

3 egg yolks

Finely grated zest and juice of 3 lemons

## FOR THE MERINGUE:

3 egg whites

175g (6oz) caster sugar

**This is a bit of a cheat's lemon meringue but I doubt anyone will complain once eaten.**

1. Preheat the oven to 190°C, fan oven 170°C, Gas mark 5.

2. Unroll the pastry and roll a little thinner. Use the rolling pin to lift the pastry to line a 20cm (8in) non-stick ovenproof frying pan. Ease the pastry into the frying pan being careful not to stretch it. Cover in cling film and place in the fridge to chill for 30 minutes. Trim once chilled.

3. Line the pastry case with parchment and fill with baking beans. Bake for about 15 minutes, remove the beans and parchment and return to the oven for a further 5 minutes. Leave to cool while making the filling and meringue.

4. **For the lemon filling:** pour the condensed milk into a bowl and whisk in the egg yolks, lemon zest and juice. The mixture will thicken but may loosen again as soon as it is stirred. Pour the mixture into the cooled pastry case.

5. **For the meringue:** put the egg whites into a large, spotlessly clean, grease-free bowl and whisk, preferably with an electric whisk, until soft peaks form when the whisk is removed. Start adding the caster sugar, a spoonful at a time, whisking well between each addition and with the electric whisk at full speed. Whisk for at least 5 minutes once all the sugar has been added. Feel a bit of the mixture between your fingers; if the mixture still feels gritty, keep whisking at full speed until all the sugar has dissolved and the mixture is smooth, stiff and glossy.

6. Spoon or pipe the meringue over the surface of the filling, making sure the filling is covered. Bake for 15–20 minutes, or until the meringue is pale golden. Set aside for at least 1 hour to allow the filling to firm up before serving.

# NUTTY CHOCOLATE CHIP COOKIE

125g (4½oz) unsalted butter

70g (2¾oz) soft brown sugar

150g (5oz) caster sugar

1 large egg

1 large egg yolk

150g (5oz) plain flour

1 tsp baking powder

Pinch of salt

125g (4½oz) dark chocolate chips

75g (3oz) pecan nuts, chopped

**Made and cooked in the frying pan so no mixers, no bowls, no baking trays – you will need plenty of willpower though, as they are absolutely delicious.**

1. Preheat the oven to 180°C, fan oven 160°C, Gas mark 4.

2. Place the butter in a 24cm (9½in) non-stick ovenproof deep frying pan and melt over a medium heat. Cook for about 3 minutes, stirring frequently until it begins to turn golden brown. Whisk in the sugars.

3. Remove the pan from heat and allow to cool for about 7 minutes. Add the egg and egg yolk. Do not be tempted to add the eggs too early or the eggs with scramble. Whisk gently until well combined. Add the flour, baking powder, and salt, stirring until just incorporated. Fold in the chocolate chips and nuts.

4. Spread the dough in the pan using a spatula. Bake for 18–20 minutes until the edges begin to turn golden brown and a toothpick inserted into the centre comes out clean. Enjoy served warm and cut into wedges with ice cream, or with a cup of tea or glass of milk.

# ACKNOWLEDGEMENTS

When I embarked on the journey to create this book all the ideas were in my head. I knew what I wanted to share but had no idea how long it would take nor how much work was involved in transforming those ideas into usable, interesting and, more importantly, tasty recipes. Well, I can tell you it took a lot of work and a lot of frying pans, but more significantly a lot of support.

First of all, I'd like to thank to my little family for their patience. To Steve for his belief in me, his encouragement and his late night dashes to the supermarket. Jac (aged 4 ¾) for his colouring in skills that were used extensively during this time. Steve and Jac were often faced with a choice of three or four dinners after I'd spent the full day testing, and would always taste obligingly (when I am sure sometimes they craved a simple pasta and pesto!).

I have worked with the very talented food photographer Toby Scott for more years than both of us would like to admit and it's always such fun. He makes the process so easy and it never feels like work, I trust him completely to create beautiful photographs and working with him on this book was a pleasure as always. Thanks to prop stylist Rebecca Newport for finding so many beautiful frying pans (not the easiest of briefs) and to Simon Smith for letting us use some of your Kempton and boot sale finds.

To Lydia Good at Penguin Random House, thank you for giving me this opportunity. She believed in this book and guided me gently through the process in her calm serene manner.

Some people helped me by eating, some helped by looking after Jac, some just helped by sharing their enthusiasm and excitement – thank you everyone, however big or small your contribution.

# ABOUT THE AUTHOR

Photo © Davina Paterson

**Mari Mererid Williams** is a seasoned food stylist and recipe writer. Starting her career with Tesco and the Seafish Industry Authority, Mari then took the helm as food editor of a couple of magazines including *Asda Magazine*. Now working as a freelance food writer and stylist, she has contributed to many of the foodie favourites such as the BBC Food website, Waitrose and the *Weekend Daily Mail*.

Mari is a go-to consultant for many of the staple food brands found in your larder, be it concocting delicious versions of classic dishes, making modern twists on favourite recipes, or creating innovative new ways to use ingredients. Mari's recipes are accessible and easy to follow; her partner Steve often acts as kitchen apprentice by testing the usability of her recipes and making them foolproof.

Mari has contributed to and styled many recipe books over the years but this is her first complete book. *One Pan, 100 Brilliant Meals* was born from her desire to inspire everyone to discover what is achievable with just one frying pan.

She lives in Hertfordshire with her partner Steve and the light of her life, her son Jac – aka Sous chef!

# INDEX

1 3 5 7 9 10 8 6 4 2

Ebury Press, an imprint of Ebury Publishing,
20 Vauxhall Bridge Road,
London SW1V 2SA

Ebury Press is part of the Penguin Random House group of
companies whose addresses can be found at
global.penguinrandomhouse.com

Penguin
Random House
UK

Mari Mererid Williams has asserted her right to be
identified as the author of this Work in accordance with the
Copyright, Designs and Patents Act 1988

Copyright © Ebury Press 2018
Photography by Toby Scott
Food styling by Mari Williams
Design by Louise Evans
Editor: Lydia Good

First published by Ebury Press in 2018

www.eburypublishing.co.uk

A CIP catalogue record for this book is available from the
British Library

ISBN 9781785037696

Printed and bound in China by C&C Offset Printing Co., Ltd.

MIX
Paper from
responsible sources
FSC® C018179